DOWNSIZING
The Blended Home

DOWNSIZING
The Blended Home

WHEN TWO HOUSEHOLDS BECOME ONE

Marni Jameson

STERLING
New York

STERLING
New York

An Imprint of Sterling Publishing
1166 Avenue of the Americas
New York, NY 10036

ISBN 978-1-4549-3473-8

Distributed in Canada by Sterling Publishing Co., Inc.
c/o Canadian Manda Group, 664 Annette Street
Toronto, Ontario M6S 2C8, Canada
Distributed in the United Kingdom by GMC Distribution Services
Castle Place, 166 High Street, Lewes, East Sussex BN7 1XU, England
Distributed in Australia by NewSouth Books
University of New South Wales, Sydney, NSW 2052, Australia

For information about custom editions, special sales,
and premium and corporate purchases, please contact
Sterling Special Sales at 800-805-5489 or
specialsales@sterlingpublishing.com.

Manufactured in Canada

2 4 6 8 10 9 7 5 3 1

sterlingpublishing.com

Cover design by David Ter-Avanesyan
Interior design by Christine Heun

For Adam, Alyssa, Brett, Paige, and Marissa

Contents

PART FOUR: How They Did It

PART FIVE: The Crazy Quilt Family

Introduction

Hearts May Become One, but Houses Collide

"Why is it your furniture and my stuff?" DC asked.

"Stuff," I thought to myself, was actually putting it nicely.

DC and I were in our fifties, and had just gotten engaged and bought a house. We were now negotiating the rocky territory of whose furnishings and housewares would go and whose would stay.

It turns out that his question was just the beginning of many good questions (and a few arguments) that arose as our hearts—and our households—not so seamlessly became one. Experts later told me that these turf wars shake the core of even the most stable relationships.

As is the case in four out of ten marriages today (according to a 2014 Pew Research Center analysis), DC and I were both remarrying. Among the many differences between getting married or moving in together in your early twenties for the first time and marrying, remarrying, or cohabitating later in life is that you have more stuff.

When you're young, you blend your bookcase made of pine planks and cinder block with your sweetheart's stained, hand-me-down sofa and beanbag chair, and build from there. More mature unions bring to the merger two dining room sets, two collections of holiday decorations, and two vacuum cleaners.

One look at the statistics showed that DC and I have plenty of company. Marriage and remarriage are thriving in America, and brides and grooms are older on average than ever. Remarriages—and thus the rate at which more established households are merging—are at a historic high. Back in the sixties, most marriages were one-and-done deals. Only one in five marriages ended in divorce. Only 13 percent of those who divorced or who lost a spouse got remarried. Today, the divorce rate hovers around 50 percent. In two out of five marriages, at least one partner has been married before. In one out of five marriages, both partners have been married before, as in our case. Older Americans are leading the trend: half of previously married seniors have tied the knot again, according to the 2014 Pew report.

Today's couples are also waiting longer to say "I do" for the first time. According to a study by the US Census Bureau in 2018, the average age at first marriage in the United States is 27 for women and 29 for men. That's up from ages 23 and 26, respectively, in 1990, and 20 and 22 in the 1960s. These statistics don't account for all the mature committed couples blending households.

All this means is that today, by the time two established adults walk down the aisle—whether for the first, second, or fifth time—they very likely have two complete households in tow: homes full of belongings that reflect who they are and where they've been, their style, and their history.

They bring to the mix belongings they worked hard for and have become attached to, an often sizable collection of material possessions that entwine with the stories of their lives. Multiply that by two, and you can see why when you merge you must purge. The math goes like this:

1 house + 1 house must = 1 house.

That means each partner must downsize by roughly half. Ouch! That is a lot of letting go. Though the merger math is simple, applying it is not.

And that is why, all across America, as hearts and homes become one, couples are saying what I said to DC: *"Darlin', I love you. But your stuff, not so much."*

MERGER IN MIDLIFE

Like so many couples marrying and remarrying, DC and I weren't just starting out. I was a divorced mom forging a new life after my marriage of 24 years ended. DC had lost his wife of 27 years to cancer and had a lot of living left to do. Our combined family of five grown children, then ages 21 to 35, were out of the house. My two were in college, and his three were forging their careers and starting families.

Though battered by the storms of life, we still believed in love, and we both, fortunately, had the nerve to drop a line in the water and try online dating.

DC, who'd had a good experience with his marriage, was more optimistic about finding a partner. I was less hopeful and more skittish. I thought the possibility of finding that special someone who would appreciate and understand my many quirks while also meeting my must-have criteria was about as likely as finding a Nordstrom on Mars.

Still, at the prodding of my two daughters, I nervously ventured onto a dating site. Shortly afterward, my profile surfaced as one of his matches, and he sent me a message.

We met on a Sunday afternoon in the spring of 2014 over a glass of wine, a date that lasted four hours. Fourteen magical months later, while standing in the empty kitchen of a four-bedroom Mediterranean-style house in Winter Park, Florida, that we'd just signed the papers on, DC proposed.

I thought my feet would never touch the ground again. However, as we discussed blending our respective homes along with our considerable collection of lifelong possessions, my feet not only touched the ground, my heels dug in like a pair of farm plows.

I, for one, was bringing more to the joint venture than a trousseau and a hope chest. DC wasn't traveling light, either. We both had entire households, belongings we'd acquired over half a century of living and raising families. We both had many cherished possessions we would need to sort through, vet, part with, and blend in a way that not only looked good, but also felt good, and felt fair.

We were fast discovering that when two houses become one, something's got to go, and you don't want it to be the relationship. Downsizing two homes to blend into one can either lead to an ugly turf war, where a clash of styles leaves behind a tsunami of hurt feelings, or a harmonious blending that lets each person shed and evolve, and that brings out and blends the best of both.

The challenge then becomes how to fairly, sensitively, and artfully cut the combined contents by half and blend what's left of two homes into one beautiful arrangement.

I wrote *Downsizing the Blended Home* to help couples do just that.

Using the story of my midlife merger as a backdrop, I added advice from experts, and tales from others who have made it through the transition, to write this book, a torch that will light the way as you purge, edit, and blend to create a home that is about the best of you both, now and going forward—not who you used to be.

Welcome to the journey.

PART ONE

Merger Math:
1 House + 1 House Must = 1 House

The merger math is simple. Applying it is not. When two houses become one, something has to give, and you don't want it to be the relationship. Discover what you both want in a home before you commit. Here's how to find that common ground where you will thrive as a couple.

1

I've Got This

When DC and I decided we were going to get a house together, I actually said to him, "Lucky for you, I can decorate. Consider that a gift to the relationship." We laugh about that now, but I was serious.

While I was honestly thinking, *I've got this. I'll take this from here and you won't have to worry about it,* DC, a lawyer who can spot manipulation from a football field away, heard this: *You think I have no taste. That sounds more like a trap than a gift, and I'm part of this process, too.*

A delicate discussion ensued, beneath which lay these thoughts:

ME: *Since I'm the one who writes the home design column, and has written books on home design, and has staged many houses to help them sell, naturally this will be my job. Plus, my furniture is better.*

HIM: *Wait a second. Why do I feel as if my identity is about to be swept away in the next Goodwill truck, along with my collection of Pittsburgh sports mugs? Besides, I like my furniture, and, to* *be frank, some of yours I don't like. Take your landscape art, for instance—please, take it away.*

We both knew better than to speak our minds.

But what I did say, trying to appeal to his legal side, was: "I have actual evidence of my decorating skills. Show me yours."

And he memorably said, "I don't want to feel like I'm living in your house."

That pretty much summed it up. In that educational instant, DC not only gave voice to all the other partners in the world who feel forced into homes that don't reflect them, but also helped myopic me see the situation from another perspective—*his.*

Oooh boy. Merging our two fully loaded households was going to be like trying to park a moving truck in a mailbox. For the first time, it occurred to me that this wasn't going to be as simple as putting what I liked where I liked.

MAKE ROOM FOR THE RELATIONSHIP

Though the dynamics of every blended home are different, one fact is constant: Whether two people are moving into a place new to both of them, as we were, or one partner is moving into the other's home, both parties need to down-size—unless one party is coming to the relationship with nothing but a backpack—or resentment will build. Plus, letting go of stuff, metaphorically speaking, shows you are letting go of the past and making room for the future; in this case, the new relationship. If one partner is moving into the other's home, for instance, the incumbent needs to do a lot more than move his or her clothes over to make space in the closet. You are remodeling your life, and your home needs to reflect that.

While moving into one partner's existing home is often the best choice for practical reasons, when both parties move into a new place, they have the advantage of working in neutral territory. In our case, while we were both moving into a new house, the living situations we were moving out of were very different.

I had already gone through a major purge—several, actually. I came to our "together house" after having moved six times in four years. I had pared down, lightened up, and purged all I could bear to spare. I pretty much thought I was living like a monk.

My first move was out of a large family home in Colorado. As my marriage was unwinding, I needed to look for steady work during the recession. I found a reporting job at a newspaper in Florida. My oldest daughter was off to college in Texas. The younger one came with me to finish high school.

We moved to the Sunshine State in spring 2011. Because trying to sell a big house in the recession was pointless, we rented out the Colorado home to a family who wound up buying about a third of the furniture. My then husband took some of the furniture to his new place, and I brought the rest to Florida. That right there cut my load by 60 percent.

In Florida, I fell into an arrangement where I became a live-in home stager. In exchange for good taste, extreme neatness, and flexibility, my daughter and I lived in various high-end properties that I would stage with my furniture to help them sell. In return, I got greatly reduced rent and didn't have to sign long-term leases or take on another mortgage.

After the initial move to Florida, I would change houses five more times before moving into what would soon become known as the Happy Yellow House.

When DC first called me in March 2014, I was in the middle of moving from my third staging project to my fourth. Because I needed to pack, move, and unpack a 3,500-square-foot (325 sq m) house in under forty-eight hours while keeping both places show-ready, I asked if he would call back in a few days, after the move.

Fortunately, he did.

Every time I moved, I purged. Knowing that I was living in a house for sale and that the next move was imminent, I would ask myself: *Do I really want to haul this box again? Do I really need these books I've already read, and these baby blankets, now that my girls are in high school and college?* By move number five, I did not have a single belonging that I hadn't carefully considered ditching.

DC, on the other hand, had lived in the same house for eighteen years—a house he had shared with his late wife and their three now-grown kids. It was packed with the stuff families collect over the years: hundreds of photos;

closets of clothes that weren't his; his daughter's dancing awards; his son's soccer trophies; and his late wife's sewing, baking, crafting, and gardening supplies. It was as if they were all still there.

He knew that when he met the right woman, she would not want to live in that home, with all its connections. But he also wisely realized he didn't want to buy another home before meeting the next Ms. Right, because he figured she'd have her opinions.

And she did!

WHERE ARE WE GOING?

The first question couples need to answer after *Do we make this move?* is *Where are we going to live?* Circumstances often dictate that one party move into the other's home, which has a series of dynamics that moving into a home new to both does not have. We'll look at both.

However, whether you rent a house or apartment or buy one, looking for a new place together—the place you will share—is the first step in envisioning your new life together. The home you choose will literally shape how you live. Think about what features you want that will nurture you as individuals and as a couple, and choose thoughtfully.

House Hunting in the Hypothetical

*O**ne year after that Sunday afternoon glass of wine . . .*
"I am not a house snob," I said to DC.

He raised his eyebrows, lowered his chin, and regarded me over the top of his glasses. After a year of dating, DC said he wanted to sell his house and move on. He wanted to go house hunting—with me—but thought pleasing me might be a tall order.

"Okay," I continued, "so maybe I'm what some might call *particular*, but that's just because I have a point of view."

DC stayed wisely silent. His lips formed a doubtful seam. Thanks to his legal background, he's well trained in the art of choosing battles and seeing where arguments will lead, which I am not. I tried to look at it from his viewpoint.

I guess I couldn't blame him. If I were dating a home design columnist, author, and stager who had also built and designed three houses, I might find the prospect of looking at houses with this person a bit daunting, too.

If I were also contemplating buying a house in which said home design columnist just might possibly, Lord willing and the creek don't rise, live in—with me—the situation just might cement my shoes to the sidewalk.

On top of that, when DC asked me to go house hunting, I had a hunch that beneath the invitation lay a thinly disguised marriage proposal. Being the traditional types, we both had said that if the right person were to come along, we would like to remarry. Neither of us was interested in just living together.

DC knew that the way to my heart was through my home. I had already fallen for him; once I fell for a house, I'd be a goner.

He also knew me well enough to know that I could not resist an invitation to house shop. I love sizing up properties and getting a voyeur's view into how others live. I also like to look at houses and dream, just a little, about another life I might possibly live.

Sure, I could keep living my vagabond life as a human prop, with a perpetual lockbox on my front door, or I could be open to the prospect of a wonderful stable home with a wonderful stable man.

"I don't want you to have to go through that again," DC said after my sixth move to a new staging project, possibly the nicest thing anyone has ever said to me— which is how we found ourselves sitting together on the sofa surfing realtor.com before tackling the bigger question of *our future together.*

DC, whom I fondly refer to as Mr. Two Steps Ahead, started many conversations with one handy word that made everything less scary: *Hypothetically.*

"Hypothetically speaking, what part of town would you like to live in?" Or, "Hypothetically, what size house would be ideal?" Or, "How do you feel about having a home theater, hypothetically, of course?"

Hypothetically became our code for if stars and hearts align, and the heavens smile, and the kids get along, then, maybe, a house, maybe, together.

Hypothetically, what's to worry about?

We toured dozens of homes online, selecting those in a 20-mile (32 km) circle around our respective workplaces. The "discussion" typically went like this:

DC: *"What do you think of this one?"*
ME: *Nose wrinkle.*

Without ever leaving the sofa, we surfed through houses in a wide range of sizes and prices. We dialed in likes, dislikes, musts, and must nots, and learned more about ourselves and each other in the process. And I learned that when buying a house to accommodate a new life and a new start with a new someone, begin online. This lets you stay emotionally detached—at least from a property.

This is the time to ask yourself and each other what features you're looking for in a home. Create your must-have list and your would-like-to-have list before seeing properties in person.

WHAT DO YOU WANT IN A HOME?

After you set your price range, talk to each other about the following factors (hypothetically speaking, of course). All these considerations will greatly affect your quality of life together. Then make a checklist.

- **SIZE**. Picture your new life together, and how much room you will need to support it. How small is too small? How big is too big? Both sizes can backfire. Be thoughtful.
- **LIFESTYLE**. What activities do you each love and want your home to support? For example, do you enjoy gourmet cooking, entertaining, movie watching, reading, or gardening? Do you need to work from home? Do you require a mother-in-law suite?
- **ROOMS**. How many bedrooms and bathrooms do you collectively need (really need) and why?
- **PETS**. If either of you has animals, how will the space accommodate them? Will they need a fenced yard or nearby park?
- **URBAN OR SUBURBAN**. How important is walkability to you, or proximity to work, culture, shopping, and restaurants? Conversely, how important to you are open spaces, views of nature, and getting more house for less money?
- **SCHOOLS**. Even if you don't have kids in public school, being in a neighborhood with good schools is important for a home's resale value, and also speaks to the values and stability of its residents.
- **COMMUTE**. How long is the drive or train ride to work? If you commute to work or school, try to pick a place that

makes the trip as short as possible for both of you while still meeting other housing criteria.

- **STYLE.** How important are looks to you? Your home should make you feel happy when you drive up. Does the home have great appeal, or can you give it some?

Make a Checklist

Here's what our checklist looked like. Yours might look very different, but the point is to make a list together and talk about what matters in your home.

- **CURB APPEAL.** I wanted a place that made me happy when I pulled up. If I didn't get that good drive-up feeling, I didn't even want to go in.
- **CHARACTER.** Many homes lack character. I wanted a non-cookie-cutter house with a distinct architectural style.
- **ENOUGH BEDROOMS.** Together DC and I have five grown kids. Two were married and just starting families. We expected all would come visit and stay, but not necessarily all at once. Yet, we didn't want to maintain a home with rooms we would only use at most two-thirds of the year.
- **A NICE, NOT-TOO-BIG YARD.** I wanted to plant some flowers, and have room for DC's dog, Peapod, and maybe one more, but not a yard so big that we'd become hostage to it.
- **A WELL-TENDED STREET.** Part of a home's appeal is what's around it. If the prospective house has great landscaping but the other yards on the street are dumpy, it's a nonstarter.

- **A TERRIFIC KITCHEN AND GREAT ROOM.** These two spaces are the heart of the home, and we both envisioned big gatherings of family and friends here.
- **DEDICATED SPACES.** I wanted a place for a home office. DC wanted a room where he could play guitar.
- **A HIDDEN GARAGE.** This is just me, but I prefer a house you don't drive into, thus a garage entry either perpendicular to the street, or behind the house.
- **A SEPARATE DINING ROOM.** We both wanted a dining room that didn't look into the kitchen.
- **AN OUTDOOR EATING SPACE.** No matter how much my kids complain about it, I still love to eat outside when weather permits.
- **A HOUSE THAT ENTERTAINS WELL.** A home is for living in, and having family and friends over is living at its best.

HOUSE HUNTING LIVE

Eventually, we put away the laptop and got into the car. So began a standing date. Once a week for several weeks during a long lunch hour, we looked at houses with DC's real estate agent, Wendy.

Before each session, Wendy would email us links to contenders that fit most of our needs. Seeing all of them was not possible, as the list was full of mixed signals: big yard for the dog; low-maintenance landscape. We'd tour each home online first, ruling out many. If the house didn't have photographic appeal, promise, and potential; was geographically undesirable; or had obvious chronic issues, we hit delete.

Eventually we winnowed candidates down to a handful to see in person.

This process is exactly like online dating, we agreed. Because we had found each other online against all odds, we had some faith, but we also knew that not every person or every place is as advertised. Like much of life, the house-hunting process turned out to be a string of butterfly-high hopes followed by canyons of disappointment. Houses with so much promise online turned out to have fatal flaws—literally. One faced a cemetery.

The in-person house encounters were also a lot like many first dates—demoralizing. Nonetheless, each week, we climbed into Wendy's SUV and toured a handful of homes.

Many houses that DC liked, I nixed. "I like a broader range of houses than you do," he said (his diplomatic way of saying I was a picky pain in the posterior).

True, I eliminated prospects swiftly: ceilings too low, character lacking, price too high, too much work, funky flow, cheap finishes, outdated everything. Just like dating.

DC was more generous. "What's wrong with this one?" he asked about a house he liked.

"It's too brown."

The more we looked, the more specific the criteria became about what we (okay, mostly me) were looking for. And then we found it.

THE HOUSE THAT GOT AWAY

I knew the minute I found "The House." It checked all the boxes. And then it got away. I hadn't been this heartsick since I got sent home from summer camp with mono.

On one of our weekly house-hunting escapades-slash-therapy sessions, Wendy drove us by a sunny-colored Mediterranean-style house that had just come on the market. I craned my neck so hard as we drove past my head almost came unscrewed. The house oozed charm. What's more, all the houses on the street were equally delightful. Wendy made an appointment for us to see the house that Sunday.

I arrived before DC. The listing agent was there, and had opened the home to show other buyers, too. As I walked through the door, a warm fluttery sensation started at the bottom of my stomach and branched up like an electric tree through the tips of my ears. I later deconstructed this gestalt to be a cocktail of the warm, butter-colored walls, dark hardwood floors, substantial plantation shutters, 10-foot (3 m) ceilings, crown moldings, wrought-iron balusters, granite counters, and harmonious marriage of exterior and interior architecture.

Whoever had chosen the finishes had a sure hand and good taste, and knew better than to take a shortcut. By the time I walked through the kitchen and great room to the enclosed brick courtyard out back, where a fountain was softly burbling, my knees could barely hold me up.

Just then, DC walked in. "What do you think?" he asked.

My eyes turned into twin Ferris wheels. Then I put a finger to my lips. Another buyer was walking through the house with her agent, and I didn't want to tip our hand.

Outside on the sidewalk, we huddled with Wendy, and within minutes told her to submit an offer. I was giddy on DC's behalf, and, hypothetically, on mine. That night, Wendy called. The house had sold.

"Sold?"

"Before I could submit the offer," she said.

"What? How?"

Apparently, the other buyer who was there called her husband after we left, and before Wendy had a chance to write up and submit our offer, they swooped in with an offer the sellers accepted on the spot.

"Will they take a backup offer?" I asked, groveling.

"No," said Wendy, "the deal was solid, full price and all cash."

Tears welled. My heart fell fifteen floors. I tried giving myself a "meant-to-be" pep talk, which didn't work. They never do.

"Houses are like buses," DC said, consoling me as I mopped a pond of tears. "Another one always comes along."

"But *that's* the bus I, I mean, *you*, I mean, *we*, want."

Two days later, Wendy called. The cash deal had fallen apart. The selling agent wanted to know if we were still interested in the Happy Yellow House. By that evening, we had a deal.

"ONE OF THE MOST EXCITING PARTS OF MY JOB is when I see those lights click on," said Atlanta-based broker Rhonda Duffy, one of Georgia's top-selling agents, about the moment buyers know.

Having recently experienced one of those "this-is-the-house" moments, I was fascinated by how homebuyers can make such a life-altering decision in minutes.

"Eighty-eight percent of buyers know within the first five minutes," said Duffy, who has sold nearly twenty thousand homes and has seen that phenomenon often. "Buyers have a vision of what they want to live in."

And with whom, I wanted to add.

"They can't always articulate it, but they have a picture, a combination of where they've lived and their experiences," she continued.

"House buying and relationships are inseparable, and the right house changes with the seasons of your life," she said. For instance, young professionals with no kids often want an urban townhome, close to work and city life. Newlyweds might want a fixer in a good neighborhood that they can remodel and maybe make some money on. New parents often want a larger home in a safe suburban neighborhood with lots of other young families; they are willing to trade a shorter commute for a larger house. Mature adults and empty nesters often want less house with low maintenance on a well-tended street within walking distance to shops, theaters, and restaurants, and room for guests or for the kids to come home now and then.

"You knew instantly because you both had done your homework and had a vision. When you saw what you'd been looking for, you could pull the trigger."

Moreover, I had already imagined DC and me in the kitchen together making dinner, then watching a movie in the great room, while the dogs (there would be two) dozed in the courtyard on a warm summer night. I had already moved in—in my mind, anyway.

Indeed, DC and I had visualized together, created our wish list, pictured our life together, and what that would look like, and found not my house, or his house, but our house.

HOW TO KNOW IT'S "THE HOUSE"

If you want to experience that knowing feeling next time you're looking for a house, retrace these steps, Duffy recommends:

- **MAKE THAT WISH LIST.** Beyond price range, location, and number of bedrooms, include must-haves and would-be-nice-to-haves. Topping the list might be plenty of space between you and the neighbors, a gourmet kitchen, or a front porch.

- **START ONLINE.** But surf with caution, warns Duffy. Seeing pictures of a house online is great, but you miss what the neighborhood looks like. Online looking doesn't replace being there, and you also risk ruling out a gem because it didn't photograph well.

- **GET ON THE SAME PAGE.** Because buyers are usually couples, both need to merge their visions. This gets interesting, she says. "Talk about your wish lists, look at pictures together, and create one vision."

- **LOOK FOR MASSIVE VALUE.** Massive value isn't about price, Duffy says. It's about what is really important to you. The couple selling the Happy Yellow House had three young boys. They valued more space indoors and out. I valued high-end amenities, and walkability to restaurants, theaters, and shops.

- **RATE HOUSES FROM ONE TO TEN.** If it's a seven or higher, check out the neighborhood. Eliminate any house under seven. Typically your front-runners will have the top two or three wants on your wish list, but not all.

- **BE READY TO BUY.** Good houses priced well go fast. (We know.) And you may not want to wait for the next bus.

BEFORE YOU BUY, CHECK UNDER THE HOOD

The dog barks day and night. Dealers sell drugs on the corner. The neighbor plays drums and tuba. The garbage dump is just over your back hill. The flight path to the nearby airport barely clears your chimney. The homeowners' association fines you every time you leave your garage door open. Construction seemingly goes on day and night.

If you'd only known. . . . The wrong neighborhood can kill the romance fast.

Hard as it is to find a house you love in your price range, that is not enough. You need to love the hood, too. Because you don't just buy a house, you buy everything around it.

"The number one reason people move—besides downsizing or upsizing—is because they don't like their neighbors," says Duffy.

Her advice: Get to know the neighborhood before you sign the mortgage docs. Find out, literally, what you are getting into. Here are questions Duffy says to ask before you sign the dotted line:

- CRIME. Ask neighbors about crime in the area. Look on the neighborhood app Nextdoor. Also look online at police reports, and check websites that list registered sex offenders to see if any live nearby. "Buying a house is an emotional decision, and the first emotion everyone needs to feel is safe," says Duffy.
- SCHOOLS. Ask the neighbors how many school-age children are in the neighborhood, how the schools are, and where the bus stop is. Go online and look up how the schools rate. Good schools and good neighborhoods go together.
- TRAFFIC. Ask the neighbors whether traffic poses a safety issue. Also inquire about noise from cars, trains, or planes. Turn off any masking noise, such as music or a water feature, and listen.
- NOISE. Ask the neighbors about any other noisy nuisances like barking dogs or chronic partiers. "Moving next to loud neighbors who don't share your desire for peace and tranquility will create friction fast," she says.
- HOMEOWNERS' ASSOCIATION. If an HOA governs the community, ask neighbors about its culture and reputation, and how often it cites residents and for what. "If the HOA fines you every time you leave your trash cans out a few hours too long, you don't feel safe. You feel

violated," Buffy warns. Get a copy of the bylaws and read them. Find out what the dues are, and what they cover.

- **WHO'S WHO.** Ask the neighbors who else lives on the street: professionals, young families, empty nesters, college kids? Most homeowners seek like-minded neighbors.

- **TRANSIENCE.** Ask your agent—or a representative from the HOA, if the community has one—how many residents rent. If homes on the street are for sale, ask why the sellers are moving. Renters aren't as invested in their property as owners, and neighborhoods in flux are less stable. Inquire whether any of the homes are available for short-term or vacation rental.

- **ACID TEST.** Finally, ask the neighbors whether they know of any reason you shouldn't buy the house you are interested in, and, if they had to do it over, whether they would buy the house they are in.

"When people go looking for a house, what they are really looking for is their vision for their future," said Duffy. "It requires a leap of faith."

Agreeing to co-buy the Happy Yellow House with DC felt like Commitment with a capital *C*. Thirty days later, right after we'd signed the papers, DC and I went to the empty house, which was now ours. There, he opened a kitchen drawer, pulled out a little box, and asked if I would marry him.

YOUR PLACE OR MINE?

Although merging into a home that is new to both of you— one that you choose together and that allows you to begin your shared vision—is ideal, it's not always practical. The situation often requires one partner to move into the other partner's home. Maybe one person rents, so is more mobile, or maybe one partner has school-age children and doesn't want the kids to change schools. Maybe one partner's place will better accommodate the couple by virtue of its size or proximity to work. Regardless, when this arrangement makes the most sense practically or financially, partners need to be very aware of the sensitivities on both sides, and the difference between redrawing the lines and crossing them.

Whether you are the crasher or the crashee, you need to see the shared place as both of yours, said Dr. Amanda Miller, associate professor of sociology at the University of Indianapolis, and coauthor of *Cohabitation Nation: Gender, Class, and the Remaking of Relationships* (2017). In other words, incumbents need to do more than just make room in the closest and clear out a bathroom drawer.

"What works best is when the incumbent is willing to tear everything down, and to see nothing as sacred," said Miller. "Strip everything down and start over. Take every picture off the wall. Put it all out on the front lawn and decide together."

In other words, start from scratch. When you do, you will need to confront the question of how the person moving in can put his or her imprint on the other person's home, said Miller, adding that research shows that couples are equally likely to move into the woman's home as into the man's. "We've found no gender dynamic." What matters is that the person whose space is being moved into no longer views it as only his or her place, but as the couple's, according to Miller. (You'll see in chapter 20, however, why good theory and real life often aren't the same.)

What also matters is that couples share an understanding of the terms of their living arrangement. In her studies on couples living together, Dr. Miller and other sociologists have identified three categories of couple cohabitation in addition to traditional marriage, which is still the most common. Miller describes them like this:

- The alternative to being single and dating. You're not sure this is your forever relationship but you like the person, and living together is more convenient and financially advantageous.
- The alternative to marriage. You don't want to ever get married, but want to be together for the rest of your lives.
- The precursor to marriage. This couple intends to get married someday.

What matters is not the model you choose, so much as making sure both parties are on the same page and agree on what their relationship is and where it is or isn't heading. Unfortunately, she says, many couples are not intentional about moving in together. Another common mistake people make is they creep in. One week they start leaving their toothbrush at their partner's house, and pretty soon it's their clothes.

"By far the most satisfied couples are those who spell out what the arrangement is going to be, down to the chores," Miller said. "If couples don't have those conversations, friction builds, and you end up with a lot of resentment."

3

When Redesigning Your Life, Redesign Your Home

Within a day of getting engaged and buying a house—two heart-stopping events that happened in one day and might trump the day I turned sixteen and got my driver's license and a puppy—I got right down to what mattered.

I made a scaled furniture plan.

Using quarter-inch graph paper, I drew a floor plan of the Happy Yellow House. Then I cut out to-scale pieces of furniture, which I slid around the plan until I liked where they landed, and I glued them down.

This is like paper dolls for grown-ups. I was in house heaven. For four years, my inner home designer had been on mute while I staged homes in "neutral and universally appealing ways" to please others.

The chance to finally decorate my own home made me feel like a racehorse set loose after a long trailer ride.

Poor DC. He had no idea how much pent-up decorating mojo lay roiling, ready to erupt.

"I made a floor plan," I told him, hauling out my graph-paper mock-up.

"What took you so long?" he said. I sidled up next to him and talked him through each room.

"What's this?" He pointed to a furniture patch.

"My blue sofa."

"And this?"

"My kitchen table."

"Where's my furniture?"

I paused. "Oh, your armoire is here, and your glass console . . ."

But I now saw what he saw: my pieces outnumbered his, ten to one. "Actually," I said, trying to recover, "a lot of your stuff is here, you just can't see it."

"Like what?"

"Well, your knives. We are definitely going with your knives. And your wineglasses, and definitely your Tupperware®. Your Tupperware rocks."

He continued to mull the furniture plan.

"You don't like it," I said.

"I'm sure it will look great," he said, "but I like a lot of my furniture, too."

As with so many scenarios in life, I never saw this coming.

"When my kids come to visit, I want them to see parts of their lives here, too," said DC, sounding like the perfectly reasonable person he is. I then did something rare for me. I got quiet and did some thinking, which sounds kind of like a spoon in the garbage disposal. What I thought was this: I'd gotten so carried away in all the excitement, I forgot one key part. I wasn't designing my home. I was designing *our* home.

I needed to rewind, regroup, and call Dr. Toby Israel, a design psychologist from Princeton, New Jersey, whom I check in with when I have a design question that's also personal. I should probably have a standing appointment with her. Israel is the author of *Some Place Like Home: Using Design Psychology to Create Ideal Places* (2003). She also conducts design psychology workshops.

"Blending households is a big issue," said Israel. "Although on the surface you're talking about furniture or fabric or color or rooms, the conversation is really about the relationship itself. While you're trying to blend decorating styles, you're really trying to blend two lives."

"Geesh, I thought blending families was the hard part, not the furniture."

"Moving furniture is really symbolic," she said. "The driving question becomes: How are you going to combine the best of two people in a way that is nurturing and satisfying for both?"

Read that sentence again.

"Here I'm focusing on whose dining room table would look better, his or mine (*mine!*), and it never occurred to me he'd want input," I said. "Besides, this is what I do."

"It's a mistake to think that you have the answer because you're a professional." Okay, that felt like a donkey kick.

"Remember what you're after," she said. "You want a happy home with your partner, not carte blanche to do what you want."

"I kind of want both."

FIND YOUR SHARED VISION

Fortunately, my mock plan spurred a healthy discussion with DC about what our new blended home would look and feel like. We agreed on a few design points at least, in the abstract, and then Israel weighed in on our progress. Here's what we discussed:

PICK A STYLE. Like family members, all the furniture in a blended household should ideally get along. My furniture was mostly traditional, specifically Old World European with French influences. DC's was a mix of contemporary, American traditional, and Southwestern. After talking about which of our belongings would get along, and which ones we'd like to come home to, we agreed on a transitional look: a decorating style that would blend traditional and contemporary, and would bridge our belongings while building a fresher look. (We'll talk more about finding your style in chapter 7 and combining styles in chapter 8.)

ISRAEL SAID: "Perfect. You came up with a shared vision."

FRAME THOSE PHOTOS. As a live-in home stager, I was not allowed to display personal photos because it prevented buyers from seeing themselves in the home. Thus, I'd already packed mine away and gotten used to not having them. DC's home still had shelves full of family photos accrued over decades. We wanted *our* home to make both of us and all our kids feel at home—but at *our* home, not a relic from either person's past. We agreed we'd have one table of well-edited family photos that represented everyone equally, and we'd tie the photos together by placing them in coordinating frames. (We'll talk more about family photos in chapter 16).

ISRAEL SAID: "Your photo table says it all: Everybody has a place here, and we're all coming together under the same frame."

MAKE A FOLDER. I had started a design folder of inspirational photos, and paint and fabric swatches. While initially the folder was meant to guide me, the visuals helped DC and me talk about what we wanted home to be. I handed him home design magazines and asked him to pull out pictures of interiors he liked.

ISRAEL SAID: "To get that high, positive association with home, you need to discover what home is for your partner and tap into that."

LOVE FIRST. Although this sounds forehead-smackingly obvious, trust me: When you want your coffee table, and your partner wants his, horns can lock. Whenever I found myself feeling a standoff coming on, I used this mantra (maybe I am getting mushy in my middle age): "Love first."

ISRAEL SAID: "That's the right lens. You don't want to be right but not happy."

WHEN A COFFEE TABLE IS
NOT JUST A COFFEE TABLE

As we tiptoed into those treacherous waters, I decided to do a little more investigating about what all was going on behind our fight for our stuff, to find out why a coffee table can be more than a coffee table.

The movie *When Harry Met Sally* has a scene where two characters, Jess (Bruno Kirby) and Marie (Carrie Fisher), are moving in together. Jess wants his beloved wagon wheel coffee table in the living room, as it reminds him of home, and he cannot understand why Marie thinks it's so awful.

They look to Sally (Meg Ryan) and Harry (Billy Crystal) to take sides. Sally wrinkles her nose and gives a little head shake, but Harry reframes the whole scenario and puts the maligned coffee table into the context of the bigger relationship, noting that it won't really matter in the scheme of things.

When I saw this movie in the theater, I still remember the audience's reaction, the knowing laughter. Everyone in that theater seemed to identify. Later, I began to better understand the undercurrents of this scene, which really wasn't about the coffee table at all, but about feeling that what matters to you is represented in your house.

As DC and I were gearing up for our big merge, I continued to look to experts who had ventured before us. I had more talks with design psychologist Israel, and with Seattle designer Rebecca West, who specializes in transitional design—designing through life transitions. Both believe that when you redesign your life, you should redesign your home, too.

"When you live alone, you want to design an oasis that nurtures one spirit," Israel said. "When two lives merge, you want a sacred cave that protects them both."

In her design psychology workshops, Israel often talks with couples who are working on blending their lives and homes. The process brings all sorts of issues to the surface, including issues of security—*Whose house is this? If it's yours, where do I live?*—and issues of personality; extroverts see the home as a place to gather, while introverts need a place to be alone, she said. It also raises issues of what each individual needs to be emotionally safe.

And then there's the common conflict of one partner liking the house neater than the other. Shortly after DC and I started talking about getting married and merging our households, I raised a warning flag. He saw how my home looked. As a live-in home stager, nothing was out of place. The homes I lived in were show-ready from 10 a.m. to 6 p.m. every day. That was not only my job, but also how I liked to live. I mentioned this to him because he evidently didn't share the same need for a tidy home.

I said, "Darlin', I don't just like a neat and tidy house, I *require* it for my mental well-being." He quickly deduced that what I meant was that his way of piling things all over the kitchen counters, desks, and dressers wouldn't fly in my—err, I mean, *our*—home.

"I don't want to be a nag, but what am I supposed to do when your stuff reaches my breaking point?" I asked him.

"You just say, 'Uhh, DC,' and point to my mess," he said.

"Agreed."

(When you're marrying someone who negotiates for a living, having these discussions up front helps.)

I told Israel about this conversation, which she applauded. "You were expressing your need, and that is good. You said, 'I need order or I can't think straight' and that's giving the person an understanding of who you are. The deeper you go with these issues, the more you learn."

These discussions, whether they involve furnishings or lifestyles, are tricky, yet essential, she added. "You're oriented to the aesthetic and the visual; he's responding to the symbolism of things reflecting his past. To him, having lots of stuff around gives him a feeling of purpose and industriousness. You can use these discussions to learn about each other."

The way a home is decorated tells you a lot about the relationship between those who live there, she said. "What you see on the surface reflects what's going on below the surface."

She's particularly attuned to spaces where one party is overly dominant. Homes where one partner "owns" more space than the other or where one person's style overpowers and marginalizes the other's should send up a flare. Typically one partner (usually, though not always, the woman) is given or takes the lead in the decorating, and that person is charged with making sure the home taps into what everyone who lives there needs in order to feel "at home." A place where the homemaker has created a home that is all about her, with no expression of the husband or his kids, is not a place that will foster a nurturing nest kind of feeling.

Israel once worked with a couple in Upstate New York. They had just married and were blending a family. She was moving into his house, which he liked as it was; he didn't let her have any input.

"Though she was helping pay the mortgage, he never put her name on the loan or the title," said Israel. "As we got into it, I told her she was in a vulnerable position, and she needed to bring up not only the idea of who owns what, but also to bring to the couple's consciousness that she had the right to be represented in the home."

Israel also told me of a friend of hers who had moved into her boyfriend's house, where he had lived for twenty-four years—most of them with his now ex-wife. The friend didn't mind the decor, except that most of it was selected by her "predecessor." He thought the house was fine as it was and didn't see the point of spending money on new furniture. "My friend never felt she was part of the home, and the relationship didn't last."

In these cases, a couple needs to work together to redesign the house to reflect their redesigned life, Israel explained. This is especially important if one partner has shared the house with a previous partner. "The incumbent has to be sensitive to how that feels for the new partner and make it safe for the new person."

But the resident often doesn't see the problem. "Often the person who lives there sees everything as just fine, and doesn't want to spend money to redo the place," said Rebecca West, author of *Happy Starts at Home* (2016). "But by not remodeling with the new partner, you prevent that person's spirit from coming in."

DESIGNING THROUGH TRANSITIONS

"When working with couples, I like to make sure both voices get expressed," said West. By going through her own marriage, divorce, and remarriage, West unwittingly became an expert in transitional design, and came to believe that decorating is the best therapy. A former ballroom dance instructor, she parlayed her life transitions into a niche design business. "Re-creating my space actually helped me through," she said. She now helps clients redecorate their homes as they remodel their lives.

"When couples remarry, if one of the voices is muffled in the design process, that won't work. Both need to come along on the adventure."

I, of course, was listening closely.

"When we remarry as [mature] adults, the challenge is to thoughtfully blend belongings in a way that supports where the two of you are going and let go of the people you are leaving behind," she said.

As we chatted, I realized that if I had I known West before now, together we would have burned through more boxes of chocolates and tissues than a sorority house during rush.

Her design work, which she calls transitional, caught my attention because I was interested in interior design that bridged traditional and contemporary styles. Only, when I looked closer, I saw that wasn't the kind of "transitional" she was talking about. She meant designing through *life's* transitions.

Now I was really interested.

In 2007, West's seven-year marriage came to a painful end. She got the house. "But I felt like I was suffocating in it. All around me were the remnants of this failure: the paint colors we picked together, the poster we both loved that hung over the fireplace, the burgundy sofa that was a hand-me-down from his family, the bed. . . . I couldn't afford to move."

"There was only one thing to do," I said.

"REDECORATE!" we said in unison.

West traded out the greens and burgundies featured in her married home for pinks, purples, and robin's-egg blues, hues that marked her new single life. She hung a feminine painting over the fireplace. She sold the burgundy couch on Craigslist for $100 and bought a turquoise one for $30. She ditched the queen bed and got a twin. "I turned it into a feminine dollhouse," she said, exactly what she needed just then.

"Redecorating through transitions is about using your space as a tool to figure out who you are and where you're going," she said.

Told you decorating is therapy.

Eventually, West found the courage to remarry. Next, her job was "to create an interior that was less man-repellant."

Since remarrying, West rented out her home, and worked with her second husband, in a place new to both of them, to create a fresh space that reflected both. She blended the blues she found so soothing in her single home with masculine browns.

"The question for this new relationship and this new home was how do I show up here and have this be about him, too?" she summarized. "It's its own wonderful."

MINDFUL MERGING

Homes aren't static. Kids come and go, in-laws move in and out, couples become singles, and singles become couples. As households expand and contract, their decor should evolve to support and reflect what is, and what is to be, not what was. Here are tips from West and Israel for those in transition:

- **MOVE ON, NOT OUT.** The key for anyone in transition—for instance, those shifting from a "my" house to an "our" house—is to focus on the next chapter, not the last one. Remodel your home so it supports the person you're becoming and doesn't force you to live in the past.

- **PICTURE STARTING FROM NOTHING.** To help you visualize your best life now, imagine, worst-case scenario, that your house burns down and you must start over. What would you add back? This forces you to become very intentional about what you want in your life, according to West.

- **COLOR YOUR WORLD.** Color is the biggest mood influencer, and easy to change. If you want to transform a space from me to we, the fastest, cheapest way is with paint. (More on color in chapter 11.)

- **LOOK FOR GOOD CONNECTIONS.** If a piece of furniture or art reminds you of a negative time in your past, ditch it. Surround yourself with items that reinforce positive feelings.

- **FIND YOUR MUST-HAVES**. Whether suddenly single or newly hitched, look around you for the five or so nonnegotiable items that ground you—items that tether you so you're not adrift. Give those a place in your remodeled space and build on them. (More on touchstone pieces in chapter 6.)

- **GET YOUR PRIORITIES STRAIGHT**. If you're merging households and finding resistance, ask yourself what's more important, your relationship or the furniture? If you care about the relationship and the other person cares about a chair, let him or her keep the chair. "Staying selfish is the most common mistake people make in this situation," West notes. "They forget that they're trying to create something new."

- **THINK FORWARD, NOT BACKWARD**. Creating a home together is about what you're trying to build, not what you want to hold on to. Focus on the future.

- **HAVE COMPASSION**. You may never understand why your partner is so attached to his recliner. But to him it's where he's watched all those great games since college. At his core, he feels that if you reject his chair, you're rejecting him. Try to appreciate what certain belongings might mean to your mate.

- **RESPECT FEELINGS**. Similarly, if something really rubs you the wrong way, even if it's irrational, express your feelings. Maybe your new beau has a stuffed animal from his ex-girlfriend on the bed. It reminds him of his childhood dog, but it reminds you of her, and every time you come into the bedroom you grind your teeth. That item needs to go.

- **DIG DEEP**. Ask yourself why you are putting up such a fight. Is it because he won the last argument, and now it's your turn? Or because she's not throwing away enough, in your opinion? A fight about the sofa—or a wagon wheel coffee table—is often not about the sofa. Identify and address what's really underneath the disagreement. (More on why couples disagree in chapter 6.)

- **GET PRACTICAL**. If one person's a neatnik and the other has packrat tendencies, as was the case with us, create a defined place—preferably out of sight—with some shelving for the clinger to put things, within reason, Israel suggests. In other words, accommodate without enabling.

- **SHOW, DON'T TELL**. Verbal language is often not enough when trying to communicate interior design visions, West says. "I've seen one partner say, 'I'd like a blue room,' and the other person recoils. But show that same person a picture of what you mean by a blue room, and they like it." West asks couples to go on Houzz.com and to each choose photos of ten rooms they would like to come home to. Then she compares the images and finds that often, partners aren't as far apart as they think. "By staying in a verbal place and not a visual place, you can create arguments that don't need to happen."

- **MAKE ROOM FOR THE KIDS**. If kids are coming along on the move, even if they only stay part time, they each need a space that's theirs, Israel advises, a place they can feel is their place in the family, both physically and emotionally. "This place serves as their metaphor, and answers their question of where they fit into the family." (We'll talk more about the kids in chapter 16.)

- **DRAW IT UP**. Before placing the furniture, create a floor plan. Think in terms of private, public, and semiprivate spaces, Israel says. Do a work plan to see that both of you are represented. Identify areas you both will share, as well as private spaces.

- **AVOID THE TABOO.** Every new relationship has old baggage. For couples remarrying, the bags are bigger. The old marital bed is one charged item, as are family photos of the former spouse or partner. A new bed is ideal, and new bedding is a must. One couple I spoke to also felt that replacing the silverware former spouses had used was necessary. Photos of past partners don't have a place on the walls in the new home, adds West. "Put them in an old-marriage box or in a file on your laptop." That way you preserve the past chapter while honoring the new one.

- **CONSIDER IT AN INVESTMENT.** Oh, and let go of the idea that you're wasting money when you replace items you think are fine, West notes. "Get something new together and consider it an investment in your future." (See more on this in chapter 10.)

- **BEING RIGHT IS RELATIVE.** Furniture that works in one home doesn't automatically belong in the next. I learned this through my multiple home-staging experiences. DC also came to realize this during our blending process. For instance, although he was fond of his Southwestern lamp with a Kokopelli base and tin shade—which looked right in a room that had a Southwest motif at his old house— when I asked him without judgment where he saw it in the new house, he was able to let go.

"When a whole room is done, it's the perfect combination of elements playing well together," West explains.

"You might not have chosen that wall color, or this particular rug, but the way the ingredients relate to each other just works." Kind of like the two of you.

In later chapters, we'll talk more specifically about mixing furniture from two households so that it "gets along," but the first step to moving in together is to move out. At least one partner, if not both, will need to pull up stakes. This is when the downsizing to blend begins, and it is a perfect time to reassess what does and doesn't belong in your life moving forward.

RIGHT AFTER OUR OFFER ON THE HAPPY YELLOW HOUSE was accepted, the home I was staging sold and went under contract, which was perfect timing. Now our focus turned to cleaning up DC's home, getting it sold, and deciding along the way what would move with us and what would not.

It was time to roll up our sleeves to sort, purge, and merge.

PART TWO

Moving Out

Before two people move in, one, if not both, must move out. The downsizing begins here. If one partner must sell a home to move on, these professional staging techniques will help land a fast sale at top price, and clean house in the process.

4

To Sell Fast at Top Price, Stage Like a Pro

Chances are, in order to move in together, one or both of you have to move out. If you're renting, you're a step ahead, because you can cut and run. But if you own a home that you need to sell, getting it ready for market is an excellent time to reassess your stuff and make that first big cut. A home that is pared down to its essentials, that is decluttered to show it has room to spare, and that is well staged will sell faster and for a higher price than the same house brimming with stuff and wearing that well-lived-in look.

Naturally, I not only wanted DC's house to sell quickly so we could move onto our happily ever after, but I also wanted him to get top dollar. In short, I was motivated. Meanwhile, my current staging project, the home I was living in, had just sold. With my staging record, his sale shouldn't take long.

But this staging project was different.

When the idea of staging his house to sell came up, DC, who had watched enough HGTV to know, was already tuned into the power of staging. He had also watched me, in the fourteen months he'd known me, stage three very different houses to help them fetch top dollar.

DC admittedly didn't have the faintest idea how to take his Florida home from lived-in domesticity to gotta-have-it desirable. So he agreed to stand back and let me have my way with the place.

Yet applying my clutter busting and decorating skills to his well-lived-in place, we both knew, would be a job fraught with peril. This was no ordinary sale for him, no typical staging project for me. The house was loaded, in every sense.

DC knew he couldn't stay in the home he'd shared with his late wife if he wanted to move on, which fortunately he did—with me. So here we were.

"I wouldn't want another woman to live in that house, and neither would she," he told me when we first met on that Sunday afternoon over a glass of Sauvignon Blanc.

Though two years had passed since my divorce and his wife's death, the events still seemed recent. DC and I were tiptoeing warily forward.

WE STARTED AT THE CURB with a clear, unclouded eyes. DC held a yellow legal pad and a pen poised to take notes about what needed to be done to get his 2,400-square-foot

(223-sq m), four-bedroom, single-family, one-story home with a pool ready for market, and, more significantly, sold fast at a great price.

Let me interrupt this account to say: dating does not get easier in middle age. If anything, it's more complicated. In your twenties, what do you have to deal with, really? You likely don't have much in the way of kids, real estate, stretch marks, 401(k) plans, former spouses, art collections, or dental work. You don't have decades of baggage, or the vaguest idea what an HDL to LDL ratio is, let alone what yours is.

"I plan to remulch," DC said, bringing me back to my senses. Yes, where was I? It was so easy for me to drift from curb appeal to matters of the heart. I never could discern the line between home life and home design.

We scanned the landscape together.

"Good," I replied. "We'll put some brightly colored flowers in these pots." I pointed to the twin lifeless urns flanking the front door. "Give the front entry a good cleaning." I drew a streak in the film on the glass of an out-door carriage lamp. "And replace the doormat." We looked down at the worn-out WELCOME on the mat.

The outside decisions were easiest. As we stepped over the threshold, I took care to check my straight-shooting self at the curb. I'm a Westerner and a journalist. My say-it-like-it-is approach doesn't always play well here in the kinder, gentler South, where politeness prevails and locals beat around the bush so much they sometimes never get out of the hedges. In the Southeast, my directness can go over like a sledgehammer on a dandelion.

I'm working on this.

DC held his pen a little tighter, his pad a little closer, bracing. I did my level best to tread lightly as I went room by room calling out changes, trying not to hurt the feelings of anyone, dead or alive.

This was for sure: After nearly two years of bachelor living, the home needed a woman's touch. Fortunately, DC had already done most of the exterior, man-of-the-house improvements. He'd recently had the roof replaced, the pool resurfaced, and the patio area power cleaned. With the structure in good shape, we now needed to focus on the background, or "shell," as they say in the business. Once walls and floors were in good shape, we could start staging.

As we made our way, my advice began to sound repetitive: declutter, depersonalize, deep clean. I looked at DC frequently to assess his color, like a medic checking vitals. The patient was holding up well in stable condition until I said *repaint and recarpet*. At that point, he stopped breathing.

We had only just begun.

READY, SET, GO TO MARKET!

Regardless of whether the home for sale is yours or your partner's, the steps to getting a property market-ready are the same:

- **LOOK AT YOUR HOUSE LIKE A STRANGER.** We all have blind spots when looking at our homes. Try seeing yours as if for the first time. Also, invite someone honest and objective, such as your broker or a friend with good taste, to tell you how a buyer would see it.

- **TAKE CARE OF STRUCTURAL ISSUES.** If the roof leaks, the plumbing needs repairing, or the rain gutters are falling, fix it. Make sure the house is sound and in good repair; otherwise, you are inviting a lowball offer.

- **CREATE GREAT CURB APPEAL.** If the house doesn't look great on arrival, it won't matter how nice the inside looks. Curb appeal is the first impression, and it is hugely important. Force yourself to see cobwebs in the eaves, grimy windows, and dirty walkways or decks. Power clean the exterior. Do what you need to do to make your brown lawn green. Spruce up neglected planters with fresh mulch and seasonal color. Place colorful pots of flowers by doors. Paint the door if it looks tired, and replace the hardware. Clean and repaint outdoor light fixtures so they gleam.

- **UPDATE THE SHELL.** If floors and walls aren't in good condition, paint, recarpet, and refinish floors. Remove dated and dirty window treatments. Avoid the temptation to offer buyers a carpet or painting allowance. That's lazy. Buyers have enough to deal with, and don't want to add getting carpet to the list (see pages 46–48). Create a turnkey house.

- **STAY NEUTRAL.** Paint and carpet with neutral, coordinated colors. Choosing colors from the same strip of a paint sampler will assure they share an undertone and work together. Choose carpet that is one shade darker than the walls and nothing darker than a midtone.

Before he met me, DC had painted his dining room Sherwin-Williams® Bagel, a warm tan that looked terrific. But he veered from that palette when painting the great room Certain Peach (a pinkish-salmon color) and the hallway Snowbound (a greige off-white), which looked jarring. We toned those areas down and repainted them another color on the same strip as Bagel, a shade called Interactive Cream, which gave the interior cohesion.

With the structural repairs and the shell (carpet and paint) refreshed, we could forge ahead and stage to get the home ready for market.

"Can you work with what I have?" DC asked, sounding worried. He was still clutching that yellow legal pad.

"Absolutely!" I said, though I was a bit worried, too. Regardless, I sure did not want to buy more furniture for this place. We had twice as much as we needed. We were going to have to shoehorn ourselves and our stuff into the Happy Yellow House as it was.

Previously, I'd always staged with my own furnishings. Using someone else's was going to take more, uh, creativity. But redecorating with DC's furniture had an upside: As I rearranged his house, I became more familiar with his furnishings and their potential.

I was sensitive to the fact that DC was moving from a home he'd shared for nearly two decades with his late wife and three now-grown children. I knew that everything we touched detonated a memory. But this was business.

DON'T LEAVE IT TO THE BUYERS:
THE CASE OF THE CARPET

When I arrived at the house, the "vandals" were still there. Every drawer and cupboard had coughed up its contents, and sweaty men with tattoos were lifting heavy things and swearing. As sexy as that might sound, it wasn't.

I had come straight from work wearing a skirt and heels, overdressed for the circumstances, and carrying a bag of Chinese takeout—which was wholly inadequate given the situation. I looked past the fray and saw DC on the other side of the house. He was wearing a look of resigned tolerance and fading good humor, which was commendable considering it was his house being ransacked—for me. Only one person was to blame for this mess, and she was holding the bag.

At the heart of the mayhem was DC's fifteen-year-old carpet. He had asked me what he should do to get his house market-ready. So I told him. "Replace the worn carpet" was on the list. Now, amid the sweating and swearing and commotion, I flashed back to the conversation that had brought us to this moment.

"Are you sure I need to replace the carpet?" he asked.

"Without a doubt," I said.

"What if we just cleaned it?"

I shook my head and pointed to the indelible traffic patterns.

"But I'd have to move all the furniture."

"Oh, that's nothing." I waved my hand dismissively. "Carpet installers move furniture every day."

"Why don't I just give the new buyers a carpet allowance; let them pick what they want?"

"If you want to sell your house quickly and for the best price, you need to show it in its best light. Period. And that means no fifteen-year-old carpet."

"But what if the buyers don't like the color I pick, or want hardwood?"

"No woman—and I'm sorry, mostly women decide which home to buy—already juggling the 550 moving parts of moving, including figuring out where her furniture will go and where the schools are, wants to add 'get new carpet' to the to-do list. She sees a home with new carpet, and thinks, 'Phew, one less thing to worry about.'"

He ran this past Wendy. The same broker who sold us the Happy Yellow House was listing this one. She, being an astute reader of home sellers, saw that DC would rather donate an eye than replace his carpet, so gave lukewarm support to the carpet allowance idea.

"Wendy says I can give a carpet allowance," he said.

"Wendy wants the listing," I said.

"Okay," he conceded. The next day, before he could change his mind, I was back with carpet samples.

And this was how I found myself on the threshold of chaos, overdressed, holding the bag, doubting my convictions.

After a ten-hour installation, the sweaty tattooed men left and I helped DC put the house back together. The next day I came by, walking in softly in case he wasn't speaking to me— and I wouldn't blame him. The carpet looked fantastic.

"That was rough," he said, "but I'm glad we did that. It does look a lot better."

It's so easy and convenient for sellers to say—whether the home needs fresh paint or new carpet—we'll just leave it to the buyers to pick. Don't fall into that trap.

"First we need to remove all the stuff," I said.

"What stuff?" DC asked.

I looked at him sideways and realized he was serious. Like most homeowners, he didn't see his home with fresh eyes.

"Everything that doesn't require two people to move needs to go."

"Go where?"

"Step one, when staging a home, is to strip rooms down to the big furniture," I said. "What's in here?" I picked up a handsome wooden box that sounded as if it were filled with sand.

"The dog's ashes."

"Oh."

Though he was ready to move on, the difference between saying so and doing so was like the difference between wanting to run a marathon and crossing the finish line.

Because he'd asked me to help, I switched from my role as fiancée to professional home stager—a perilous transition. "Get rid of this, and this has to go" is easy for me to say, when it's not my place—literally or figuratively.

We started in what should have been the living room, only it wasn't.

"This room needs a purpose," I said.

"It has a purpose," he said. True, the room off the entry, which should have been a living room, had, over the years, morphed into an office/music room. It housed a packed desk, stacks of music on the floor, a piano, an electric keyboard, a guitar, and a pair of conga drums.

"Buyers would like to see this as a living room," I said. He made a face, then made a note.

I continued with my mantra: declutter, depersonalize, deep clean. Then we could decorate with a fresh eye.

"Can't we stage and *then* clean?"

"That's like putting makeup on without washing your face." He nodded as if he understood and let out a little puff of air in resignation.

We stripped each room to its basics. One vacant bedroom was converted into a landing pad where we corralled decorative items we might use in the accessorizing phase of staging or in the new house. Other items went to the donate pile in the garage, next to the fast-growing trash pile. We tagged some items for Craigslist.

DC surveyed the keep collection—figurines and photos, planter pots and pillows—and the remaining large furniture. "Show me what really matters to you," I said. He pointed to his Pennsylvania House oak rolltop desk, some Native American crafts he'd bought in Arizona, a console table and coordinating mirror made of carved limestone, a couple of paintings he'd acquired in his travels, his bedroom armoire, and his massive ten-piece dining room set. Of course, we'd use more of his furnishings than that, I promised, but these treasures would get priority in the new house. Though I had some serious reservations about his dining room set, I didn't air those yet. I hoped that keeping the items he loved most would buffer the blow that inevitably hits when you dismantle a lifetime, as I well knew.

With the rooms stripped and accessories parked in the holding area, DC brought in a cleaning crew who scoured everything from ceiling fans to baseboards. Then, at last, it was time to stage.

During one weekend of heavy lifting, I transformed— and I don't use that word lightly—the heavily lived in, mildly neglected single-family home on a shady, tree-lined street into a Florida oasis.

That Sunday night, DC hosted a party—a house sendoff—and confessed, "I have never seen my house look better." He was proud of his home, and he should have been.

Monday, Wendy came by and took pictures. Tuesday, the house went on the market. Wednesday it sold to the first buyer who walked in, for the price DC wanted.

BOOM! DONE! SOLD! In under twenty-four hours.

"Wow!" came the text from Wendy the next day. "No doubt in my mind the reason we got such a fast offer is because of all the work you did getting it ready to show. He owes you a nice dinner out."

"Nah. I'm pretty sure I'm the winner here," I texted back.

The point is this: *Staging works.*

Moreover, much of what we just did was a dress rehearsal for what was to come.

THE POWER OF THE STAGE

No matter how corny or contrived you think putting a bow around your bath towels might be, setting the dining room table all fancy though no one is coming to dinner, or putting a little black dress out on the bed, staging can make the difference between a home that turns fast for a great price, and one that sits. That's because buyers decide to buy a home based on the *feeling* they get. It's emotional. Plus, staging is practically free. I used the furniture and accessories on hand, and spent $200 total on fresh flowers, new patio-seat cushions, and a new doormat. Period. What I did to stage DC's home is a formula anyone selling a home can follow:

- **CLEAR THE DECKS.** Strip every room back to its skeleton. Remove all clutter, accessories, and smaller items. After purging what can go, park remaining decorative accessories in one central staging area, which you will later "shop." This helps you see both your space and your furnishings with a fresh eye.
- **MAKE "IMMACULATE" YOUR MANTRA.** Outside, clean all windows, doors, eaves, walkways, patios, and

outdoor lamps. Inside, scrub every surface, particularly light switches, cabinets, baseboards, blinds, moldings, grout, and appliances. I mean, use cotton swabs and toothbrushes. Kitchens and baths should sparkle.

- **ARRANGE ROOMS WITH A PURPOSE.** With each room pared to its basics, reconsider the layout. Rearrange large furniture, such as sofas, table, and chairs, considering traffic flow and function. Play up nice views and downplay bad ones. Make it easy for buyers to see how they would live there: where they would sit and visit, play cards, work on the computer, enjoy a bath, watch TV, dress for the evening, plan a menu, or have friends to dinner. This is the "suggested selling" concept restaurants use when they set coffee cups or wineglasses on the table before guests sit down.

- **LAYER IN ART, RUGS, AND SMALL PIECES OF FURNITURE.** Once large furniture is in place, add smaller furnishings back in, such as artwork, lamps, small tables or chests, and area rugs. This takes some trial and error, so take your time and keep assessing rooms with a critical and objective eye. Make sure each room does not look too cluttered or too bare. Try items and take them away until the room clicks.

- **DEPERSONALIZE.** As you purge and pare, remove family photos. One or two can stay, but generally, they are distractions. Buyers want to see their family, not yours, living there. Also, because you don't want to antagonize buyers, remove all religious or political items: Bibles, crosses, pictures of you with a politician. You never know.

- **FINISH WITH ACCESSORIES.** Now bring in throw pillows, greenery, sculptural items, and display-worthy books.

When accessorizing, go for a few large items and avoid trinkets. Select based on size (bigger than a grapefruit), height, color, and varied textures. For instance, put something low and matte like a basket beside something tall and shiny, like a blown-glass pitcher. Don't overdo.

- **REMOVE PETS AND THEIR PARAPHERNALIA.** As much as we love our pets, they are buyer repellants. Fido and Fifi need to go on a holiday while your home is for sale, and so does any trace of them, including their beds, bowls, toys, leashes, and litter boxes.

- **RUN A SMELL CHECK.** New paint and carpet will help your home smell cleaner. But you should also layer in a wonderful fresh—not cloying—scent. I avoid anything that smells of vanilla, coconut, or heavy floral notes, and lean toward citrus and herbal combinations, or clean-smelling fragrances like fresh linen.

INSIDER STAGING SECRETS

Here are my top ten staging tricks to raise your staging game to pro status (note that incorporating these tips even when you're not selling is not a half-bad way to live beautifully):

1. *The one-third rule.* When styling a bookcase or built-in shelving unit, think thirds. One third of the shelves should have books—hardcover only, please—distributed evenly. These books should not reflect any religious or political extremism. One third of the shelves should have attractive accessories, and one third should be open.

2. *Pull an accent color through.* Pick a strong color and feature it throughout the house. I chose turquoise in DC's home, because it is a good Florida color, he had plenty of turquoise items on hand, and the color tied the indoors to the outdoor pool. (See chapter 11 for more on unifying decor styles through color.)

3. *What's cooking?* Get a handsome bookstand for the kitchen counter and place a nice cookbook on it, open to a recipe with a picture of something delicious looking, as if that's what's for dinner tonight. Choose something that won't offend vegans, low carbers, or gluten-free followers, like tomato basil soup.

4. *Clear the closets.* You're moving anyway; box up and bag off-season clothing items and linens so clothing and linen closets look airy. When prospective buyers open the closets, you want to show them there is room to spare. Stuffed cupboards telegraph limited storage space. You want buyers to think, "Gee, if I lived here, my life would fall into place, too."

5. *Project affluence.* On a shelf in your closet, in which you now have room to spare, set a shopping bag from a high-end store with tissue poking out. It telegraphs to buyers that if they lived here, they too would be able to afford the finer things in life.

6. *Project luxury.* Splurge on fresh flowers. I bought a live orchid for the great room, a flowering plant for the kitchen table, and more bright flowering plants for the outdoor pots. Live plants and fresh flowers convey that living things— plants, people, and pets—will flourish there.

7. *Project a modern lifestyle.* Get rid of anything that smacks of old technology, including landline telephones, wires coming out of the walls, and intercom systems.

8. *Project good times*. Set the dining tables—indoor as well as outdoor, if you have a patio—so it looks as if company's coming.

9. *Project happy, healthy kids*. Hang a party dress in the girl's room, or a volleyball and team jersey; park a baseball bat and glove in the corner of the boy's room, or a guitar.

10. *Project romance*. Put a silky nightgown on the bed or hang one on the closet door. Put two flutes of champagne and a bottle of bubbly and some chocolates on a tray beside the bed. I know it sounds goofy, but trust me, it works.

The home-staging process offers several advantages. The house for sale has never looked better. You've teased probably 40 to 60 percent of the stuff out, or at least got it into the garage. You and your partner have both seen how good the place looks with less. And you've shown each other how great life can be when your environment is detailed and thoughtfully designed.

WITH MY HOUSE-STAGING PROJECT SOLD, DC's house sold, and the Happy Yellow House becoming ours, our train tracks were merging. We were excited about the future. But we also knew we had only a few weeks left to decide what would find a home in our new house, and to find a new home for the rest. Although DC thought he'd made significant progress in the downsizing process—and he had!— our mutual downsizing had only just begun.

5

Ouch! But It Hurts to Let Go

During the days ahead, the great purge continued.

"Clearing out my house with Marni's help is like being a soldier at Valley Forge under Baron von Steuben," DC bemoaned to his dog, Peapod. She's heard the story of the Revolutionary War hero before. She looked at me with sympathetic eyes. "I'm doing this for your master's own good," I explained to her. "He needs to shed, like you do. He doesn't need fourteen coffee mugs with sports logos. Besides, we need to make room for my mugs, too."

"Like Steuben," DC continued, "Marni takes the concept of discipline and ruthless efficiency to a new level. You watch or she'll give away your food bowl."

"Oh, Peapod, you know I would only do that if you had two of them." I gave her head a good rub.

"I can only keep four sports mugs?" DC asked incredulously. We didn't have time for discussion. DC needed to be out in less than a week. While we were thrilled by the fast sale, the buyers wanted to take ownership in four weeks, and during two of those weeks, DC had to be out of the country. Meanwhile, I had my own house to pack up, and we both had full-time jobs. We were down to the wire. A military intervention was in order.

Though he had handed down truckloads of furniture to his grown kids, the house was still crammed to the rafters with layers of past life. I'm always amazed at how a family home can continue to cough up its contents for days, like a kid with the croup.

From the attic to the closets, Christmas decor, craft supplies, table linens, and school memorabilia poured out alongside vases, platters, and candles (forty-five pillar candles alone, which we cut to ten). For DC, every cupboard detonated a small explosion of memories.

I tried to tread lightly. Again, this was not my place, literally or figuratively. Still, despite my efforts to maintain a poker face, I could occasionally feel a nostril lift.

"Did you see Marni's nose wrinkle, Peapod? She doesn't like my coffee table." Peapod's brown eyes locked on DC's with interest, hoping he would say something worthwhile, like *pepperoni*. "But just like you," he said, scratching her chin, "Marni has given me a new way of looking at life."

DC invited his kids over to take one more look at all that was left of their family home and pick what they wanted. Then he called the Sharing Center to pick up a truckload of goods he was donating.

When I saw DC the morning his old house was scheduled to pass into the hands of the new owners, he was wearing the same dress shirt and slacks he'd worn to work the day before, and a weary look.

"Did you sleep?" I asked.

He shook his head. "I worked through the night, and I'm still not done." Now, I don't know anyone who plans better than DC, but he seriously underestimated how long the task of clearing out his family home would take. Most people do. "It was brutal."

The vision of our new life together kept him going. However, as much as DC was looking forward to moving on to a new house and marriage, closing the door on the home he'd shared with his wife and kids for eighteen years was a huge undertaking—emotionally, mentally, and physically. And much of that process he had to do alone.

CLEARING A HOUSE, CLOSING A CHAPTER: DC'S TIPS FROM THE FRONT LINES

For those of you sitting on a stuffed suitcase of a house (one you have to sit on to close), a house that you have lived in a decade or more, and particularly for those of you who are about to move on and in with a new special someone, I asked DC to share here what he learned that might benefit others.

- **TRIPLE YOUR ESTIMATES.** "I way underestimated the time it would take to cull, pack, and move," he said. "I should have tripled the time, the number of boxes, and the number of trips to the donation center."

- **DON'T PROCRASTINATE.** "I knew I was a pack rat and had accumulated too much stuff. But I always thought, Why deal with it? There's time. I would now say take any opportunity you have to get rid of excess stuff, often. Don't let it mount."

- **START LOW, AIM HIGH.** DC started by clearing items that were not emotionally charged, like kitchen appliances, and then worked his way up to more loaded belongings, like his late wife's clothes. Even working through the tough stuff wasn't as bad as he feared. "You discover that what you thought was Mt. Everest, which you're not ready to climb, is really the Appalachians, hills you can hike all day."

- **GIVE FAMILY MEMBERS A CHANCE.** DC had his kids put stickers on what they wanted. "That took away any question of, for instance, whether my daughter wanted the cake pans," he said. "My kids were far less sentimental than I thought they would be. I learned a lot from them."

- **CLOSE DOORS BEHIND YOU.** DC tackled his house a room at a time. When he emptied a room, he closed the door. That served as a metaphor for closing a chapter of his life behind him, while helping him visualize progress, and focus on the finish line—the fast-approaching closing day.

- **STOP CLINGING NOW.** "So much of what we think is important isn't," he said. "Did I really need the program from the 1994 World Cup Soccer game in Orlando, or my ticket stubs from the KISS concert in the 1990s? No, but I had them. I have learned how unimportant most stuff really is."

- **TAKE COMFORT IN THE WRITE-OFFS.** DC used software called ItsDeductible™, an Intuit TurboTax® program, to track and value items he donated. Quantifying his tax deduction, coupled with the good feeling of donating to the Sharing Center, which his church supports, took much of the sting out of letting go.

- **KEEP MEMORIES, NOT STUFF.** "Going through everything I had put my life into focus and helped me crystallize memories that were murky," DC said. "It made the good memories sharper, while the less important ones faded. It also taught me this: You don't need the stuff to remember the life."

WHY WE CLING

As you and your partner pare down your pasts to begin your future, understand that the degree to which either of you has trouble letting go is in no way an indication of a lack of enthusiasm to move forward. A person can very much want to cling to things from the past, for reasons we'll discuss, but that does not mean they don't also want very much to move on to a new chapter. So do not take it personally. But do be sensitive.

If you're ever going to cut the amount of stuff you tow to the next house—the one you'll share with your new love, who, inconveniently, also has stuff—down to half or less, or if you're ever going to understand your partner's attachment to things and be sympathetic about their reluctance to let go, you need to know what makes people cling to their stuff like fuzz to wool in the first place.

Starting in infancy, we get attached to objects—stuffed animals, blankets, pacifiers—because we endow them with meaning; in this case, feelings of security and comfort. These surrogate objects fill in when a parent isn't available to cling to. This need often persists into adulthood, only the objects change—one hopes. (If your partner is bringing a teddy bear or a special blanket to the union, that is outside the scope of my expertise!)

We continue to endow objects with feelings, because things make us feel secure. When you understand that most things don't actually make us more secure, that they are just props on flimsy scaffolding, you can start to let go. But these bonds, though irrational, are deep-seated.

When helping DC clear out his home, I had him start with the end in mind. I had him envision our life—and things—together in the Happy Yellow House, and I had him ask of everything: *Do I see this in my life moving forward?* We did the same with my own house full of stuff.

Start with Your End Goals in Mind

Collaborating on a shared vision is one of the best ways for you and your partner to work through the process of cutting through stuff and letting go. Work together and imagine a home with the following qualities:

- Where you have only what you need, use, and love, and no more.

- Where, after everything is put away, you have storage space left over.

- Where you can park two cars in the garage.
- Where the space is not strongly about either one of you but a beautiful blend of both.
- Where you live a beautiful life together free of discordant clutter.

Beware of Excuses

We all have excuses for hanging on to stuff we should let go of. I've used all of these:

- It's still in good condition.
- It's still useful.
- It was expensive.
- *So-and-so* gave it to me.
- I might need it someday.
- I wore it to (*fill in special occasion*).
- It reminds me of (*fill in name of loved one*).
- The kids might want it.

These are bad reasons to move items forward. Nix those rationalizations and replace them with these questions: *Do we need it? Will we use it? Do we really love it?* If you can't answer yes to at least one of those questions, say good-bye. Also add one more important filter: *Does this item have a place in the new partnership? How will it serve our new life?* Remember, your goal is to build a future, not live in your past.

PART THREE

Moving In

Chances are you and your mate have different decor styles. Each of you should identify your style, and then begin to beautifully blend by building decor bridges.

6

Downsizing to Upsize

Whenever the subject of our moving in together came up, DC just smiled and diplomatically said, "That's going to be interesting."

Interesting was one way of putting it. The move was coming at us, and our wedding would take place not long after that.

Fortunately, we didn't have too much time to dwell as we had to make many of our decisions on the fly, in real time. As moving day fast approached, and though we'd sold our respective houses and had done a major purge, we still hadn't solved our math problem. The staged house I had been living in was 3,500 square feet (325 sq m). DC's house was 2,400 square feet (223 sq m). Both were fully furnished. Our new four-bedroom, three-and-a-half-bath house was 2,600 square feet (242 sq m). Question: How much house does this couple need to lose? Answer: At least one full house.

And so the negotiations began. While neither of us relished the idea of losing half a house each, we could foresee what would happen if we didn't deal with this now.

Here's what we did not want to do—and neither do you:

- We did not want to decide what we were keeping and what we were letting go of on moving day.

- We did not want to pay to haul furniture or miscellany that we were not going to need or use in our next place and that we would ultimately have to get rid of.

- We didn't want to deal with where to put an extra ton (and that's conservative) of furniture after the movers drove away leaving us to do the heavy lifting—literally.

- And we didn't—repeat after me—DID NOT want to put one stick of furniture in storage. (See page 66, but don't get me started.)

- We did not want to fall into the "for now" trap: *We'll just bring it "for now" and deal with it later.* When in doubt, throw it out needed to be our mantra.

Did we do everything perfectly? No. Did we overshoot and bring too much, just in case? Yes. The point is to use forethought and make whatever cuts you can before moving day.

However . . . I have been keeping something from you. There's one more piece to the math problem that I haven't told you about yet because, frankly, cutting a house's contents in half is hard enough. But you've come this far, so it's time you know: You actually should cut back each of your home furnishings by more than half. If the goal is to create a yours, mine, and ours home, you need to leave room for the two of you to buy a few key pieces together later.

HOARDING HORRORS: DO NOT BECOME A STORAGE STATISTIC

Today in the United States, there are approximately 50,000 storage facilities, according to the Self Storage Association, and they are more than 90 percent full. The average cost of storage is about $125 a month for a 10 × 10 foot (3 × 3 m) locker without climate control. That's $1,500 a year, and more than half of those who rent units keep their lockers for over a year. Do not become the one out of every ten households that rents storage.

While I'm on the subject, do not become a storage facility for your grown children's things, your parents' things, or the belongings of your partner's grown children or parents. If your kids have moved out, and you still have their Cub Scout or Brownie uniforms, or other vestiges of their youth, it needs to go. Have them go through their belongings next time they visit, or over Skype, and require them to either take or toss the contents. Similarly, those with aging or deceased parents are not responsible for being the family museum. You have enough stuff. Let go and evolve.

TAKE FIVE—THEN SHOP YOUR STUFF

Long before the moving van pulls up, plan, on paper, where things will go and what simply won't go at all. Well beforehand, talk and listen, bend and yield, defend and cry, argue and cool off, hug and talk some more, and keep foremost in mind why you are doing this: because you love each other—and that means everything each of you brings to the party.

"How did you two do it?" asked my friend Mark Brunetz, a Los Angeles designer and coauthor of *Take the U Out of Clutter*, when I called to get his take on all of this. Brunetz wrote the foreword for *Downsizing the Family Home*, and he and I share the vision of creating a beautiful well-edited home that is also meaningful. We also appreciate how hard it is to get there.

I told Mark that DC and I started by each taking inventory of our households and identifying five or six pieces that would break our hearts to lose. We earmarked those items we didn't just like, but that we'd bonded with beyond all reason, endowed with a storied past, and loved so much that losing them would feel like an amputation.

As mentioned earlier, for DC that was his Pennsylvania House rolltop oak desk, one of the first large furniture investments he made after he finished law school; a glass console table with a sculptural white limestone base and a coordinating mirror; several pieces of Southwest Indian art; his armoire, which housed his folded clothes; and his dining room set.

For me it was my French carved writing desk; a large oil painting of a landscape in California, where I'd lived most of my life; a marble-topped Bombay (bombé) chest; a large vintage French tapestry; and my dining room set.

Yes, the dining room sets were a problem. We both not only liked our own sets, a lot, but we also didn't like each other's. We'd both paid a lot of money for them, and we'd had lots of good times around these tables, so they were endowed with our respective histories. Every time the subject came up, we would lock horns and end up in a stalemate. So we tabled the table decision until we couldn't put it off anymore. You'll see how we resolved the matter shortly.

Meanwhile, we agreed that we would do all we could to make the other cherished belongings work in the new home, and build around them. Conveniently, my oldest daughter, Paige, was graduating from college and moving into her first apartment, so we loaded a U-Haul® with her bedroom furniture, DC's kitchenette set, and other small furniture items and housewares, and deposited it all at her new place. Then we put everything else in our hypothetical furniture and housewares store, and—like we did when staging DC's home—shopped our stuff. We did our best to regard items as neutral: not as his or mine, but ours.

Once again, I pulled out the graph-paper floor plan—the one that I had originally populated with mostly my things. And got out my eraser. I started with the largest, hardest to move items and our respective must-have pieces, and I took another run at the layout.

As the vision started to build, we were both literally on the same page; we could see where our furnishings fit—and fit together—in the new house, and could then layer in smaller items, side tables, lamps, and art from the store of our stuff. Importantly, we could then begin to see what else needed to go.

We also tried—and we should have done more of this—to voice appreciation for the belongings our partner had that we really liked and that we knew would enrich our new home.

TRADING UP

Now, we must pause here to state the obvious but often forgotten. Although this book is called *"Downsizing* the Blended Home," (italics mine), and while much downsizing must be done, in fact, you are about to enjoy a significant *upsize* and upgrade in your life and home.

When you overlay two households, place the contents of one up against the other, shake out the duplicates, and keep the best of what you both bring, you both come out ahead. So do all those who ultimately receive what you cast off, whether they be your kids, friends, or strangers. The world will be better for this. Keeping that in mind as you merge and purge will help as you take one step back to take two steps forward. You're not losing. You're gaining. You're trading up.

While most of the house would be a blend of our belongings, we also set off dedicated spaces. One bedroom would be a man cave for DC, where we would put his rolltop desk, sports paraphernalia, and guitars. I planned to carve out a corner of the great room for my desk. Another bedroom would be decorated with my bedroom furniture, a combination I liked that used to furnish the guest room in my

Colorado house. Knowing that we had places to call our own relieved some of the "giving-up" anxiety.

Brunetz seconded the idea of having dedicated spaces that each partner owns, because it "makes them feel represented."

Whenever DC and I hit an impasse, which was often, we would take a step back and hit the refresh button.

Brunetz put it in perspective like this: "When you start arguing, go back to the beginning and remind yourself why you are doing this. It's because you want to create a new life with this person. When you marry someone, you do not say, 'I want you but not your stuff.' When we choose people to be in our lives, we choose all of them. That's a great grounding point. When you feel yourself getting sucked back into fighting for your things, that is your touchstone."

Another reframing technique he recommends is for couples to become co-owners of each other's stuff. Stop thinking of the belongings as yours vs. mine. Start by changing pronouns from *yours* and *mine* to *ours*. By changing the language, you help neutralize the emotion.

"What should we do with our recliner," sounds less hostile than, "What should we do with your recliner."

Once you agree you both own it and are invested in it, even though your partner might have paid for it, you move from Team A vs. Team B, to We Are One Team. The sooner you lay the groundwork, the faster you will move through the transition, and the fewer feelings will get hurt.

So to review:

- **PLAN AHEAD.** Draw up a plan and decide where items will go long before the heavy lifting begins.

- **MAKE IT MEAN SOMETHING.** Work to incorporate what's most meaningful to each partner, and also the best of both of you.

- **REALIZE THE NET GAIN.** Remember that while you're downsizing your stuff, you're also upsizing your life.

- **KNOW WHAT'S NOT COMING.** Identify what items won't be moving forward with you and find new homes for them before the move. (More on that on pages 78–80.)

- **TAKE OWNERSHIP OF EACH OTHER'S BELONGINGS.** Agree that you both have things that matter and have value.

- **LEARN A NEW LANGUAGE.** No more talk of yours or mine; it's all ours.

- **KEEP YOUR PERSPECTIVE.** Finding a partner, especially later in life, is an amazing gift. Come at the process of blending your hearts and your homes with a feeling of gratefulness and all the other stuff falls into place.

If you don't get at least a little philosophical about this important life transition, you will end up fighting over whose toaster you're keeping. Keep in mind, shedding is how nature makes way for growth and new beginnings and gets rid of what has served its purpose.

"Just like when working with people to let go of their clutter, you have to remind them of the joy that's on the other side," said Brunetz. When both partners let go of part of their past, they are literally and figuratively making room for their future together.

As you approach this minefield of letting go to grow together, try saying this to your partner: "I know that letting go is hard. Let's agree that we're going to evolve. We'll take the very best and work from there to become our best us."

Though easier said than done, it's a good start.

Avoiding Turf Wars

When couples first move in together, the fights that we see are mostly turf wars, says professional organizer Ben Soreff, owner of House to Home Organizing. Fights often develop around stuff because when a loved one speaks about removing the other person's belongings, the conversation stops being about stuff and starts sounding like an intrusion.

"Arguments are usually about control," he explains. Similarly, when one partner says, "We don't need this old blender," the other person hears, "Why is it always *my* stuff you want to get rid of?"

That's not helpful. Instead, he offers these suggestions for making that work-in-progress place feel like home, because it is:

- **SEPARATE OUT THE SENTIMENTAL.** "Gather your keepsakes, but remember, not everything is important," Soreff says. "You can save keepsakes, but not out in the open. Those items live more remotely."
- **DON'T KEEP SCORE.** Once you separate out your must-haves, and have only neutral items left, stop tallying how many of whose items you're keeping. Then it's not a

question of ownership but rather which item will work best in your new home.

- **FOCUS ON THE FINISH, NOT THE FEELINGS.** Keep your eye on the unified style you've settled on, so discussions don't feel personal.

- **WORK BY CATEGORY.** Don't sort piecemeal. Gather and spread out all the kitchen gear or all the sheets and towels. Look for multiples. Then use this mantra: Select the best, donate the rest. Choose the best spatulas, towels, pans, and whisks, and let the rest go to a new home. When choosing between appliances, pick the newest or best model, and say good-bye to the others.

- **DO NOT THROW ANOTHER PERSON'S THINGS AWAY WHEN HE OR SHE ISN'T AROUND.** Enough said.

- **FIGHT FAIR.** If one partner is bent on keeping an item the other feels is unnecessary, ask in a mediating tone why "we" should keep it when neither of "us" ever uses it, or when you have two of them. You want both of you to agree that there's a good reason. If you agree to keep it, then ask where it's going to live. If you don't have room for it, reconsider.

- **CREATE A SYSTEM FOR NEATNIKS AND SLOBS.** In blended households, one person is often a neatnik and the other a slob. The neatnik feels put upon to create a tolerable environment, so often puts away the slob's things. Then the slob can't find his or her stuff. That's where fights start. Ideally, you want to talk about how to handle this before you move in. The neat person should be able to say, "I'm not going to throw any of your stuff out, but it is going to live over here." And create a space—a shelf, cabinet, or bin—for the overflow. The key to good organizing is to have systems and places for everything, so anyone can put things away. Set systems up from the get-go. Often, the problem isn't the couple, it's the house setup.

- **HANDLE THE HOBBIES**. Problems also arise around hobby stuff, says Soreff. Often one partner might compromise the home's aesthetic, or simply overtake it, to accommodate his or her passion, whether sewing, painting, aquariums, sports memorabilia, rock or record collections, ham radio components, or the ten broken computers or cars that the geek or grease monkey one day plans to revive. The best way to handle that is with a man cave or a she shed.

- **FIND THE SWEET SPOT**. If your partner has a lot of something you can barely tolerate, say flowered teapots or framed sports jerseys, the fix here is dosage. Haggle over how few of these pieces your partner needs, and how many you can tolerate.

TABLING THE TABLE DECISION

I promised to tell you how DC and I resolved the matter of the dueling dining room tables. We both rather fiercely wanted our own dining room tables and chairs in our new home's dining room. We were equally adamant about not wanting the other's. Like most houses, this house had only one dining room. And whose table would go there was the elephant in the dining room.

I'd be lying if I said DC and I didn't go nine rounds over this. While most of our negotiations about what furniture should go or stay ended after a good-natured and sometimes not-so-good-natured debate, the dining room table was the exception. We both thought our tables would look better in the space. We considered all of the following sensible solutions. Maybe one of them will work for you, though they didn't for us for the reasons noted:

- **REPURPOSE.** We could use one table in the dining room and the other elsewhere, maybe in the office as a desk, or as a patio table, or in a library or workroom. Though all good thoughts, we did not have a place for a second table.
- **MIX.** We could blend the sets, and use one person's table and the other's chairs. Again, this compromise sounds like great diplomacy, but in our case neither combination looked nearly as good as the tables with their rightful chairs. However, the hybrid arrangement might work with other combinations.
- **USE NEITHER.** Another equitable solution was to use neither, sell both, and buy a new set. This is only a good idea if neither table works in the new space, in which case the choice is practical. But buying a third table when you have two that would do, while fair, is wasteful.
- **CASH IT IN.** Sell one dining set and channel the proceeds into a great piece of art, centerpiece, or sideboard to use in the dining room, so both tables are represented.
- **MEDIATE.** Ask a neutral party you both respect to break the tie. Here's where talking to a designer or an unbiased friend whose taste and opinion you both value may help.

Ultimately, two strokes of fate settled our great dining room debate. When I wasn't around, DC asked his—soon to be *our*—daughter-in-law Tara what she thought. An amateur photographer with a good eye, Tara is married to DC's son Brett, and while she may favor DC's side of the family, she didn't grow up with DC's dining room table, so wouldn't be influenced by its sentimental value. She'd also been to my house and had seen my dining set, so was familiar with the contender.

When DC asked her which table we should use, she answered objectively: "Well, Marni's would look better."

DC did not share this conversation with me right away.

Meanwhile, as a way of throwing the decision to fate, I suggested that since both our houses were for sale, we ask our respective buyers whether either of them were interested in buying the dining room furniture in the house. The buyers of my house were not. The buyers of DC's house, however, were. They agreed on a fair price, and DC felt good knowing that not only was the dining room set going to a good family, but it would also remain in his old home. That sat well with him.

Then he told me what Tara had said, which seemed to settle the matter. (I knew in that instant that when we had the next tussle, I owed him one.)

Why a Fight about the Table Is Never about the Table

One way couples can help their mergers go more smoothly is by understanding their own value systems and each other's, says Dr. Michelle Janning, professor and chair of sociology at Whitman College in Walla Walla, Washington.

"Recognizing larger patterns can help explain why people have the emotions they do surrounding their belongings."

If you know what value systems are guiding you both, you can then turn that into a discussion and better articulate why a piece of furniture matters. "Talk about where you're coming from and what you're afraid of," says Janning, who specializes in family, divorce, and our material culture.

She offered these examples of value systems as they might relate to furniture:

- **THE MONEY-MINDED.** Those guided by financial values will have trouble giving up a table if they paid a lot of money for it, and so will fixate on the monetary value, regardless of current market value.
- **THE SENTIMENTALIST.** Others guided by nostalgia and sentiment will have trouble giving up the table because it was their grandmother's, and the family has shared hundreds of memories around this table.
- **THE ENVIRONMENTALIST.** Someone who keeps a keen eye on the environment and whose value system dictates that having too much stuff is bad for the planet might be inclined to not want a table at all. These people tend to have a value system that says our world is too full, and more stuff makes them feel depressed.
- **THE MOVER.** Often members of the younger generation value mobility, and don't want to be weighed down by heavy furniture the way their parents were.
- **THE FREEDOM FIGHTER.** Others might value freedom and fear commitment. Emotionally, a person may think, "If I

have a heavy table, I will be stuck living in a bigger place, and then I will need a partner, dogs, and kids."

"Unless you both can identify and communicate what's behind your feelings about a piece of furniture, you and your partner will talk past each other," says Janning. "If partners don't understand each other's values, they are working with currency that doesn't match."

OKAY, I'LL LET IT GO, BUT WHERE? EIGHT WAYS TO RE-HOME YOUR GOODS

The tale of the table brings up an important point. While letting go of beloved belongings hurts, it hurts a lot less if you know the item is going to a good home. Giving furniture to a family member, for instance, or to someone who really needs and wants it takes a lot of the sting away and can actually make you feel good about the handoff.

Once DC and I had finished the laborious process of ferreting out our to-keep items and had separated out our to-go piles, the question became, *go where?*

I had learned from my many moves and from clearing out my parents' home of fifty years that along the road of Disposal Way, the bus makes many stops where your items can get off before they hit the landfill.

Once you know what is in the to-go pile, dispose creatively. Here are eight ways to get rid of your things before parking them on the curb:

1. *Family first.* Ask family members what they want. Before DC put his house on the market, he asked his grown children, two sons and one daughter, to claim what they wanted. His daughter, Alyssa, who lived across the country in the Southwest, wanted her bedroom set, a lot of kitchen items, some linens, and the family china. So DC loaded up a U-Haul, and off he went. His youngest, Brett, and Brett's wife, Tara, who lived a two-hour drive away from us, wanted Brett's bedroom set for their baby boy on the way, as well as the upright piano. The older son, Adam, who was married with two kids and a house full of stuff, wanted nothing. That made a dent. After we cleared and staged the house for sale, DC put all the overflow in his garage, and gave his kids one last shot. Meanwhile, my oldest, Paige, was still setting up her new apartment, so she happily laid claim to more furniture and the duplicate kitchen items.

2. *Friends second.* For other items, ask around, post items up for grabs—or on sale for cheap—on social media. Give what you can to the closest possible person you know with a need.

3. *Ask the buyers.* Because the furniture is already there and the new homeowners can see how it looks, this often works out, and saves the cost and trouble of moving it.

4. *Have a yard sale.* Use the proceeds to buy something together for the new house.

5. *Put it on Craigslist.* Again, use the cash for something you both like.

6. *Re-home with purpose.* Think about who could use the items. Donate musical instruments to your church or

school's music department. Ask a theater if they have any use for vintage clothes, like old wedding dresses.

7. *Consign it.* Take desirable items in good condition to a consignment store, and get a percentage of the selling price.

8. *Donate it.* Give unwanted items in good condition to Goodwill, the Salvation Army, or a charity of your choice. Itemize what you donate. Use a program like ItsDeductible to value it, get a receipt, and write it off.

7

Find Your Beautifully Blended Style

He likes hard rock. I like pop. He likes suspense thrillers. I like love stories. He likes furniture made of chrome and glass. I like wood with character. He likes edgy art painted on airplane aluminum. I like landscapes painted with oil on canvas.

And we're crazy about each other.

Though DC is the zig in my zag, I worried about whether our contrasting tastes would clash or meld as we forged our lives and looks into one.

Knowing now, as DC so memorably put it, that he did not want to feel as if he were living in my house—point taken—I had to get a handle on what "our" place would look like.

I needed a vision. Make that *we* needed a vision, a shared view of how we wanted our new home to look and feel. Beyond honoring the must-have pieces we'd agreed to, purging duplicates, and filling out a floor plan, we needed to find *our* style, a look that would help us knit together our must-haves, vet and blend the rest, and be a roadmap to follow in the future.

Once we had our style pinned down, letting go of stuff—it doesn't fit our style!—would be that much easier. One could hope. I learned, as we went through this process, the issue isn't whose belongings you use, but rather whose preferences you acknowledge.

To start, we needed to define our own individual styles. Everyone has a style, yes—even if a person's furnishings don't fully reflect it. What you *have* isn't necessarily what you *like*. For instance, if you inherited your furniture, or bought it when your tastes were different, or before you knew what you liked, or if it's what your ex liked, or what your ex-mother-in-law picked, then your style and your furnishings may not be aligned. Understanding this can also help you loosen your hold as you move forward. "Why do I care? I never picked this anyway."

The time to find and talk about your combined design style is while you're both still working on your paper plans, and in the talking stage about what will go where. So while the moving truck is a long way off, and so is the donation wagon, look through magazines and talk about what interiors you like and why.

Knowing the style you're going for will help you filter your furnishings. I was able to let go of pieces I really liked because I could see they didn't fit our new direction.

WHERE ARE YOU ON THE DESIGN CONTINUUM?

There are four general hallmark categories on the interior design continuum: traditional, transitional, contemporary and modern:

Design Continuum

|----------------------|----------------------|----------------------|

Traditional   Transitional   Contemporary   Modern

Each of these categories is described here and on pages 84–86. Not covered are the many subcategories that all fall on this continuum, somewhere between embellished and sleek: farmhouse, rustic, coastal, ethnic, country, industrial, and mountain lodge, to name a few.

These descriptions will help you find where on the continuum you and your partner fall so you can determine which direction you both need to slide toward. For example, if you're modern and your partner is transitional, you'll meet in contemporary. The goal here is not to determine whose style wins, but to find how to bring them together. Once you figure out where you fall on the continuum, and where your partner falls, meet in the middle. If both partners are in the same category, be thankful for your good fortune. (But you will still need to winnow down your collective stuff.)

In our case, I was traditional. I had a house full of carved wood furniture, oil landscape paintings, a few antiques, and a country French vibe in the kitchen. Though DC's house had a mix of traditional and contemporary, he favored contemporary. We would meet in transitional.

Traditional

According to Beverly Hills designer Christopher Grubb— who creates homes all along the continuum for his A-list clientele—traditional interiors reflect a nod to the Old World, whether a reflection of European royalty or country life, and often include antiques or their reproductions. These spaces have heirlooms, tapestries, bergère chairs, embellished pillows, Oriental patterned area rugs, oil paintings of landscapes and portraits, and often pieces that have a history or a story. Interiors are decorated with such details as inlaid wood, hand-painted finishes, carved fireplaces, ornate frames, elaborate drapery, crown moldings, fringes, tassels, and needlepoint; often certain items are monogrammed (see chapter 15). Light fixtures are decorative, and have crystals and gilding. Accessories are plentiful, and the interiors feel luxurious, never skimpy.

Transitional

Transitional interiors are one step up the continuum toward modern. The look combines old-world pieces of furniture with contemporary designs, which have straighter lines. So you might see antique artwork in a gilded frame next to a clean-lined mid-century modern–style sofa, or an abstract painting next to a writing desk with curved legs. Rugs tend to be solid colored or geometric patterns. Furnishings can be ethnic, such as a custom armoire made from Chinese gates or carved-wood chairs from Morocco. Drapery is tailored. Transitional spaces are comfortable, with fringed pillows but in more updated fabrics. "It's a good look for those rooted in traditional furnishings, who want a fresher vibe," says Grubb. It's also a sweet spot for couples where one is traditional and the other contemporary, as we were.

Contemporary

Contemporary interiors are the next stop up the continuum; they are decidedly more modern—but not purely so. "The lines and furniture shapes are modern, but the rules relax as comfort becomes important," says Grubb. Furniture fabrics are more comfortable than those in a modern interior, and here you may find chenille or a cotton print. In contemporary spaces, color, which is largely absent in modern interiors, can be featured on accent walls or on the occasional throw pillow, other small furnishings, or in a collection of vases. However, you won't find carved wood, nor will you see a nod to antiquity. Rugs are geometric, or tone on tone. All art will lean toward the abstract, though the look also might include an ethnic piece like a tribal mask.

Modern

Modern interiors are all about clean lines. They feature metal finishes, sleek surfaces, and zero excess. Think chrome, leather, glass, stone, and highly finished wood. "Furniture is usually more sculptural and may not look comfortable," Grubb notes. "It's very Bauhaus and Le Corbusier. Spaces feel very museum-like." Modern and minimal go together. Interiors tend to be done in neutrals, black, and white. Wall color is usually a shade of white or grayish white. Color is reserved for artwork, which can be neutral or bold, but is always abstract or edgy contemporary. Area rugs, if any, are solid. Light fixtures are spare, and windows are bare or have simple blinds.

ASK THE HOUSE

So far, in discussing the factors that should influence your new blended home, we've talked about your must-have pieces and your blended design style. But there's one more influencing factor: the house itself. The house's location and architecture should also guide the choice of what will go inside. Whether it's a place new to you both, or your or your partner's current place—which you are redecorating, right?—consider what pieces fit. Regardless of what each partner has, an old farmhouse in Worcester will call for a very different set of furnishings than a suburban-tract home in Phoenix, or an urban loft in Seattle.

WHAT IS HOME TO YOU?

While discussing blending styles with a friend, Georgian designer Elaine Griffin, at a time when she was actively looking to blend homes with the man in her life, she spoke to much of this. (You'll find out how her merger went in chapter 18.) We agreed that once couples decide to merge heart and home, they need to talk about what they want home to be. This isn't a discussion solely about furniture as much as it is about how you want to live. Define your goals for your house together. Is it a private refuge, a place to entertain, or a spread for family gatherings?

Griffin is a fan of researching styles by creating Pinterest boards or pulling out magazine pictures, to find a look that speaks to both partners of the couple. "It may not be your favorite style, but it's happy enough," she told me. "Couples where one partner is super modern and the other super traditional can find a meeting ground in contemporary.

"It's okay to relax the borders," she said. "If you are a serious minimalist, and your partner is all about embellished traditional, you can mix modern and traditional, but have fewer items overall."

The key is to make sure big pieces align. "Rooms need a single style statement, so they flow and have a look, so make sure big pieces relate. However, accessories can and should be an eclectic mix of you both," said Griffin. "Incongruous pieces are your statement of unity."

This part of the process is actually fun, because you're not talking about your things specifically, but about what your future looks like. If you agree your new look needs to be urban modern or country coastal, it's easier to neutralize your belongings and say that the distressed pine table or the galvanized metal coffee table may not work for us. *Us* being the operative word.

8

Opposites Attract

Back in my college days of idealism, I wrote a paper called "From Fiction to Non-Fiction: Writing Along the Continuum." It explored writing at its extremes, from fantasy fiction to straight reporting, with stopovers at essay, memoir, humor, and opinion writing.

I did this because if I were going to be a writer, I wanted to write it all—facts, lies, and everything in between. I wanted to know the rules so I could break them. Later, I felt the same way about home design. I don't like to feel pigeonholed.

So I set out to understand the design continuum, and find out if I could draw from all of it and how. I didn't yet know how handy this lesson would come in later, but I did know just whom to ask: Christopher Grubb, whose work encompasses a variety of styles.

"Home decor runs the gamut from antique-filled traditionalism to stark modernism," he said, pinpointing the two ends of the design continuum.

"Some people find it relaxing to come home at the end of

their workday to clean lines, so they find modern interiors relaxing," said Grubb. "Others find them too sterile, and prefer their surroundings embellished by decorative arts, so veer traditional."

"Can you blend the looks?" I wanted to know. "What if one partner is mid-century modern and the other farmhouse chic?"

"Yes, but carefully," he cautioned. "I tell clients design is a language. Sometimes my client will like a piece, and I'll say that's nice, but we're speaking Italian and that's Chinese. Couples blending styles need to become bilingual."

BECOMING BILINGUAL

"Here's the really cool part," said Mark Brunetz, when I brought up the subject of blending styles. "In today's design world, it's all about the mix. Very few people are purists. While you used to find people who'd say, 'I only do Spanish revival,' you don't anymore. As people evolve— and remarry—they want their homes to evolve, too."

Nobody's design style is pure anymore. We live in a world of mixing, so you see farmhouse modern and contemporary industrial. "Not only is it right on trend to blend styles, I can't see us ever going back," he said.

His recommendation for couples blending their homes is to pick a couple of "crown jewels," the best furniture items from each camp—maybe it's her Victorian sideboard and his rustic Santa Fe bench, or a French deco coffee table and a carved wooden pew from a church in North Carolina—and build the room around those pieces.

"It makes for a beautiful start."

Sarah Fishburne, director of trend and design for The Home Depot®, agrees. "Some used to say that a home's style, whether traditional or contemporary, is what made it cohere. We've thrown that idea out. No one wants to commit to one style anymore. Our homes can move on as we do."

This is great news for those blending homes and decor styles.

THE BEEKMAN BOYS

Just as I was struggling to figure out how DC and I were going to blend our homes into one harmonious haven, I got an email from a book publicist asking if I wanted to see an advance copy of *Beekman 1802 Style: The Attraction of Opposites* (2015), a book about blending opposing styles in a home.

I asked how soon I could get a copy.

Written by very opposite and real-life partners Brent Ridge and Josh Kilmer-Purcell—the personalities behind a series of cookbooks, farm-inspired foods, a line of home goods, and a reality TV show, all named after their historic Sharon Springs, New York, farmhouse, Beekman 1802—the book celebrates opposites.

"When we first blended our households, neither of us wanted to give up anything," said Kilmer-Purcell when

I got him on the phone one afternoon. He leaned more toward classic vintage style, he said, while his partner, Ridge, preferred contemporary. "The first one to throw something away would be admitting defeat. We are both so bullheaded."

"And . . .?" I asked, pressing the phone hard against my ear.

"We didn't have the money to start over. So we figured out how to make modern and traditional work in an old farmhouse and soon found that incorporating opposites results in far more interesting rooms."

"Interesting?" I repeated incredulously. "Our stuff straight up clashes."

"Almost everyone merges households with someone at some point, or inherits stuff," he said. "Very few couples start from scratch."

"But your combinations look so harmonious," I said. "When I mix DC's collection of Native American carvings with my French pottery, or his black leather sofa with my needlepoint rug, the result looks like the back alley of the Salvation Army."

Then he said something refreshingly honest and reassuring: "If you just looked at [our] book, you would think we have this effortless great style. But you're seeing the end. It took a while for us to get there. Blending beautifully takes time."

"And negotiation," I added.

"We have a room that eight years later we're still not happy with," he said. "We're always moving stuff around."

Beekman Boys' Trade Secrets

Like many home decor books, *Beekman 1802 Style* has photos of many enviable rooms and aspirational copy, but I needed to know the *how* behind these rooms now, so I extracted the following trade secrets from Kilmer-Purcell:

- **HAVE ONE THING IN COMMON.** The trick to pulling off a combination of opposites is to find one unifying element: a time period, a color, a shape, or a type of item. Color can bond items from all time periods, from antique to modern. (For more on color, see chapter 11.) Like items, such as a collection of candlesticks from different eras and materials—Lucite, rustic wood, silver, and ceramic—will hold together. "As long as items have one thing in common, they can live together."

- **PLACE IN PROPORTION.** When blending opposites, Kilmer-Purcell uses one of two rules: the rule of one, where one item, say, a sleek modern mirror with an orange lacquer frame, becomes a focal point in a room full of subdued antiques and traditional pieces. The other rule is the 50:50 rule, where half the room's pieces are contemporary and the other half traditional. You need balance to pull off a mix of styles. Other ratios, like 80:20, feel off. A hallway in the Beekman farmhouse, for instance, has only two items: a mid-century modern table with a baroque clock on top. The 50:50 split of old and new makes the combination work.

- **BUILD BRIDGES.** When marrying contemporary and traditional decor, create visual bridges. When I asked how a modern glass-and-chrome coffee table could work in a room with a country pine kitchen table, Kilmer-Purcell suggested setting an old vintage accessory on the coffee table and a modern glass centerpiece on the pine table. Though I had been thinking about painting my country pine kitchen table something glossy to update it and help it blend into DC's more modern aesthetic, Kilmer-Purcell talked me out of it. "Don't paint anything that is a perfect example of what it should be," he said. Though he has many examples of painted furniture in his book, he said the pieces he paints are inexpensive and boring, like the cheap set of wood chairs he painted hot pink. I later reluctantly, but not regrettably, sold the pine table on Craigslist, and used the money to buy a more transitional table that was a better fit. That's okay, too.

- **START WITH HEART**. Anything can work if you love it, promises Kilmer-Purcell. What doesn't work is decorating to please others. "The more you try to decorate your house for others, the less likely it is to work," he said. "If you create a beautiful, expensive, perfectly curated room, people are going to hate it." Phew!

FROM COUNTRY COMFORT TO CITY CHIC

In addition to discovering the Beekman Boys' book, another event happened earlier that helped visually and mentally prepare me for this shift.

If you had asked me when I first moved from Colorado to Florida whether I could see myself someday sliding toward a more modern interior, I would have bet all my money on *no way*.

I had established my style. And I liked it. I had culled a collection of French country pieces, old-world European carved tables, tall dining chairs covered in tapestry, and oil paintings. It took me half my life, and much of my income, to get to that point, and I was certainly not going to start over. I truly believed one could be done decorating.

Meanwhile, the world around me was moving on, though I stuffed that thought into a manhole fitted with a cast-iron cover. I might have stayed stuck in my time capsule of style for many years more but for a three-pronged dose of change that caused me to rethink everything: a new man, a new home, and a new life.

Enter divine intervention.

In 2011, pre-DC, when I left my stone-and-wood Colorado Rocky Mountain home and moved to Florida, I brought my mostly traditional and French country furniture with me. You'll recall, I sold a third of the furniture to the family renting the house (huzzah!), and divided the rest between my then-husband, so he could furnish his new place, and me.

My haul, selected with home staging foremost in mind, included a pine armoire, a dining room table with eight tapestry-covered chairs, a writing desk (both the dining set and desk had carved, curved legs), oil paintings of landscapes, antique wooden chests, gilded mirrors, a marble-topped Bombay chest, needlepoint pillows, patterned rugs, a French tapestry, large ceramic chickens, white quilts, and toile bedding. You get the picture.

Just writing that down, I can smell the country air.

Then I learned, you can take the country furniture out of the country, but put country furniture in a city dwelling and it sticks out like a hay bale in a high rise.

The furnishings worked in my first few live-in staging projects, a succession of traditional suburban and historic homes. But my fifth house, which I got assigned in July 2014, was a new modern home at the urban epicenter of downtown Orlando—so urban, I could see City Hall from my front sidewalk. How could I make my country traditional furnishings, which were all I had—and with my uncertain future, I was not buying more—work in a slick city situation?

Adding to my anxiety, the seller wanted the place to have a modern vibe. I'd have to give my traditional country girl decor a city-chic spin, but how?

So I had another big chat/design-therapy session with Christopher Grubb, whose celebrity clients often have both city and country homes.

"I pretty much need to turn a country sow's ear into a solid-silk throw pillow," I said. "Can you help?"

"You can absolutely create a great urban space with traditional furniture," he said, which was reassuring. The trick is to add a few contemporary moves to create a transitional look. "But be careful," he warned, "that it doesn't look like a garage sale."

Moving toward Modern

Here are some of the ways I gave my traditional furnishings a citified spin. Grubb approved and added a few more ideas to my list. Note: You can reverse engineer all of these to move a contemporary or modern home toward one that's more traditional.

- **CHANGE SOMETHING BIG.** "Bite the bullet," Grubb said. "If you're moving from traditional to transitional, the largest pieces, like the sofa or headboard, need to be brought into play." (We'll talk about sofas in chapter 10.) "Don't start with something small, like a lamp, or it will look like a mistake," he added.

- **CHANGE THE ART.** Just one large piece of abstract art can inject a modern feel into a traditional setting, just as an oil-painted landscape can inject a traditional touch. You can pick up nice, inexpensive framed art at home stores like Z Gallerie, or paint your own canvas with bright splashes of color that tie into the home's decor. Better yet, pick out a new piece with your partner.

- **REDUCE WALL ART OVERALL.** To create a more contemporary vibe, cut back on the amount of art you have, says Grubb. Contemporary spaces show more surface, while traditional rooms have more on the walls. Let rooms breathe more by clearing wall space and removing patterns. Pull out traditional patterned area rugs, and put down solid rugs or let furniture sit on the bare floor.

- **BLOCK THAT COLOR.** A key difference between traditional and contemporary spaces is use of color. Traditional (country) interiors layer prints and patterns, while more contemporary (urban) homes use solid blocks of color. On my kitchen chairs, I flipped the seat cushions—which featured a needlepoint rooster on one side and a solid black surface on the other—so the solid side was up. I did the same with decorative pillows throughout the house. Solid side out.

- **TRADE FLORALS FOR GEOMETRICS**. If you do introduce a pattern, make it geometric. Put away the florals and botanicals.

- **FITTED OVER RELAXED**. Urban chic spaces are tailored, whereas country homes have a looser feel. In country homes, unstructured curtains puddle and billow and flutter. In a city space, drapes are fitted, pleated, and precise.

- **MIND THE LINES**. Urban chic interiors favor clean lines. Adding pictures and mirrors that have straight-edged frames, not carved ones, and furniture with straight, not curved, lines will make a traditional space more transitional.

- **ERR TOWARD SPARE**. Urban chic interiors have long swaths of clean surfaces, strategically punctuated by a carefully placed sculpture or vase. Traditional country interiors are more relaxed, and better absorb a plethora of books, dishes, dog leashes, and baskets of magazines.

All these moves work in blended homes, too, where the couple wants to bridge traditional furnishings with a more contemporary or modern aesthetic to find a middle ground, as DC and I were aiming to do. This exercise not only made me stretch, but also helped me break out of my design rut.

As for the new look, I rather liked it.

As DC and I created our transitional mix of contemporary and traditional furniture, we put modern pieces alongside traditional ones, creating a look that felt like a fresh start with some nods to the past—which seemed fitting.

However, as we blended our lives and our households, our belongings didn't just flow together harmoniously. Thankfully, I tapped a few experts who helped us and our furnishings find their way.

9

A Break from Tradition

"**I** like my style," I remember saying to DC. "I want to create *our* home," he said, sounding like the clear-headed man he is.

How could I argue with that?

I started thinking and began gently probing the edges of how we could pull off *our* look with what *we* had, and maybe just a little new. And so began the uncomfortable process of shedding, evolving, compromising, and shopping *together*.

What quickly became clear is that moving toward modern from a base of traditional, or vice versa, is tricky. In fact, creating what interior design professionals call an *eclectic interior*, which is a mix of styles, is the hardest look to pull off, though, they will also concede it is the most interesting. That's where we were headed.

But how, I wanted to know, how, after I'd worked so hard (and spent so much) buying furniture I loved, how could I just upend all that? I spoke about this common predicament with Home Depot's Sarah Fishburne.

"We all know someone who once decorated a room, or a house, and it stayed that way for years. Decades," she began.

"I know why," I chimed in. "Once the space clicks for someone, and we all know how much effort and money that takes, then that someone is afraid to change so much as a vase."

"These homes freeze in time," she said. "Those living in them have gotten stuck."

"Because who in their right mind wants to start over?" I asked. "Redecorating after you've done it once is like volunteering to do middle school over."

"But with just a few small moves . . ." she continued, as I took careful notes. "They—and you—can break out of a design rut."

She's right, of course. Homes, like people, must evolve. And blending homes with someone else is a great opportunity to shake up your look and refresh your style.

Professionally, I understood what she meant. Since it had been my job as a stager to make the house I was living in look current, I had to be honest when something looked passé. I had discovered the power of injecting the well-placed contemporary accent, which served me well as DC and I blended our things.

"The real beauty of incorporating contemporary into traditional is that your home can evolve as you do."

"Amen, sister."

FIFTEEN WAYS TO MEET IN THE MIDDLE

If one of you also has a house full of traditional furnishings, and your partner is pulling you toward a cleaner aesthetic, here are ways Phoenix interior designer Barbara Kaplan and Fishburne suggest that you, too, can tiptoe toward each other and not throw the table out with the chairs:

1. *Start with what's tired.* Look at your collective furnishings with a fresh eye, and see what is worn out, outdated, or broken, says Kaplan. Start there by replacing it with a sleeker version.

2. *Start small.* Injecting a contemporary rug or piece of art, or a modern lamp or sculpture, is a safe way to begin moving toward modern in a room full of traditional furnishings, but don't stop there.

3. *Trade heavy for light.* Swap large, heavy, dark pieces of furniture for pieces lighter in weight and color and with sleeker lines. Exchange something wooden, like a walnut coffee table, for something glass and metal.

4. *Keep contrast in mind.* Don't put heavy with heavy, or dark with dark. Put a Lucite chair at an antique desk. The contrast injects a more minimal feel.

5. *Switch out ornate handles.* Simply changing the knobs and pulls on a traditional or vintage piece with ones that are more streamlined can inject a touch of modernism.

6. *Paint furniture.* Transform heavy, dark wood furniture by painting it a lighter, brighter color. As you do, consider removing decorative moldings, so the piece looks sleeker.

7. *Revisit a partner's piece, and update it for the new voyage.* Re-cover a traditional chair in a modern fabric to bridge looks. (See more on reupholstering in chapter 12.)

8. *Clean up the windows.* Swap out billowy, layered, elaborate drapery and heavy valances with lighter, simpler straight-lined window coverings, or none at all.

9. *Replace embellishment with clean lines.* Elaborate frames, carved wood, fringe, and other adornments are hallmarks of traditional style. Switching those elements out for cleaner, straighter lines will refresh a space. Replace patterned fringed pillows with solid-color, clean-edged ones, and swap out ornate frames for simple ones or go frameless.

10. *Balance as you blend.* Incorporate a little bit of modern in every room, so the mix is consistent throughout the house. Pair an antique bed with modern art, a vintage chest with a modern sculpture.

11. *Pair old with new.* Fishburne put her grandparents' old Drexel Heritage® dining room table on a modern rug, a nod to her past and her present. To take her country-style bedroom from traditional to transitional, she hung two contemporary sunburst mirrors over an old brass bed.

12. *Mix old and new in one piece.* Spray-paint an old natural wicker chair a current color, like glossy, bright orange; re-cover a vintage sofa in a contemporary print; or put a sleek frame on a traditional oil painting.

13. *Mix more, match less.* "You have my permission to mix finishes," says Fishburne. Too many home decorators stay committed to one color of wood and one shade of metal. That's not necessary.

14. *Be a rug trader.* Replace a traditional Oriental-style rug with one that has a more modern pattern and color combination, or go with a solid sisal or jute rug. Transitional rugs often take a traditional pattern and blow up the scale, drop the boarders, and swap dated colors, say, burgundy and gold, for new shades like peacock and terra-cotta.

15. *Streamline the stuffy.* Switch out oversized, bulky, upholstered furniture for less stuffy, straighter-lined sofas and chairs.

FIVE SMALL MOVES, ZERO NEW FURNITURE, ONE GREAT NEW LOOK

Although DC and I worked toward a mix that would achieve a transitional look, not every room fell together. The dining room in the Happy Yellow House was one of those rooms. We'd moved in my traditional dining room table and high-backed tapestry-covered chairs, and with them came a French country open hutch, traditional rug, and a pair of round, ornate mirrors. I emailed Fishburne a photo of the room with a subject line that read "S.O.S."

I was on the phone with her as she opened the email.

To fill the long silence while she took it in, I explained: "See, when DC and I moved into the Happy Yellow House, our lives fell into place, but our furniture, well, we're still hashing that out. The dining room in particular doesn't reflect us."

More silence as she searched for something constructive yet nice to say.

"I'm hoping I can update the room and make it look more connected to the rest of the house by just changing the accessories, without . . . errr . . . buying new furniture, because my husband and I have too much as it is." I hoped she didn't think I was just being cheap (which I was).

"You absolutely can," she reassured me.

I breathed audibly.

Then together we deconstructed my dining room. "The mistake people make when inserting something modern in a traditional space is they don't go far enough," she says. "One contemporary piece in a traditional room looks like a misstep. Three to five, and the style shift feels intentional."

Here's how Fishburne and I bridged my style and DC's in five easy moves—without changing the furniture:

1. *New wall color.* By repainting the buttercream walls Sherwin-Williams Bunglehouse Blue (a marine shade of navy), I tapped a current color trend and ultimately tied the dining room to the rest of the house (which you will read more about in chapter 11).

2. *A new rug.* Fishburne approved a transitional wool rug I found that had a large-scale pattern and bolder colors, which was a welcome change from its boring, beige predecessor.

3. *Modern mirrors.* Because the dining room was small, I had hung round mirrors, rather than artwork, on either side of the window at the room's far end. Fishburne liked the

idea of round mirrors, but not the ones I had, which had ornate, carved antique-gold frames. We replaced them with more modern mirrors DC picked out, which featured chunky prism-sculpted contemporary frames finished in champagne gold.

4. *Edited accessories.* While we kept the French country open hutch, I thinned and rearranged the visible china and crystal on the open shelves, so they looked tighter and more organized: everything of a kind together, not spread out, and no pieces overlapping. That helped contemporize the space, as did replacing a dried floral arrangement and antique tray, which were on top of the hutch, with a series of large turquoise ceramic plates on stands, which came from DC's side.

5. *New light fixture.* The Mediterranean-style iron light fixture that came with the house seemed dated, but since it went with the fixtures throughout the house, I felt constrained. While matching is always safe, Fishburne gave me permission to mix metals. Switching in a champagne gold chandelier with clean, modern lines definitely helped lift the room from its rut, and DC loved it. "So often, this one change, which is easy and not hugely expensive, can make the most significant difference."

When all the changes were in place, I sent Fishburne an after photo. "Yes!" she wrote back. "This is proof that you can make a few updates, while complementing the main pieces in the room, and refresh it."

Which is just what I had in mind.

DECORATING ACROSS THE GENDER DIVIDE

Those who live alone often celebrate that by making their homes all about them and their status—single! A woman's place becomes a feminine chick nest, while a bachelor may create a masculine man pad. When these individuals start to blend, however, her floral sofa with lace pillows makes him cringe, and she recoils at the thought of his black-lacquer bar.

"Don't knock the other person's taste," said Dr. Jeannette Lofas, founder of the Stepfamily Foundation. "In blended homes, we need to respect the differences of every member. If she likes flowers and he likes leather, creatively incorporate the male and female. Get leather sofas and use a floral fabric on the draperies."

A blend in the master bedroom is especially important. If her bedroom is pink and purple, and his is burgundy and tan, a new gender-neutral color scheme is in order, designer Christopher Grubb explained. "Blue is a perfect color for a couple's master bedroom because it's male enough, still pretty, universally appealing, and restful."

A contractor who specializes in old house renovations, Sheila Ratliff had created a feminine haven all her own. "I had a great bungalow," she said of the 2,000-square-foot (186 sq m) home she had decorated with lots of antiques, pottery, and funky glass art. "I got to design it exactly how I wanted. That house was all about me and I loved it."

But she let that go when she remodeled the new home she would share with her second husband. "I was very careful to make sure Victor felt comfortable in this house. I had done a number of houses. I wanted to do this one for him."

Sheila had been single for twenty-eight years. Then she and Victor Ratliff renewed an old relationship. The two had dated briefly back in the 1980s, when they both worked for the same ad agency. Sheila was a divorced single mom of one son, and Victor was playing the field. He would marry twice before settling down with Sheila. They reconnected in 2004, bought a 2,300-square-foot (214 sq m), mid-century house in 2005, spent a year renovating it, and got married in the home—literally as the paint was drying—in 2006.

Before selling her bungalow, however, Sheila had a huge estate sale, and got rid of more than half of her furnishings and almost all the antiques ("except for those that were like family," she said), because she couldn't see them moving forward in her new life. She then worked to incorporate Victor's traditional "bachelor condo" furniture and sensibilities into their together home, starting by using a brown, beige, and greige color palette.

"I always felt very clear that our home had to be an equal amount of his and mine," she said.

Though she left her beloved bungalow, "I was very happy to sell that and move into this house and this situation," she said. Today, she and Victor, both in their seventies, call their home a fair mix of them both.

10

Big Stuff First

Personal dynamics aside, in an ideal world, every interior design job should follow the same three steps, in this order:

1. Create your shell (floor, walls, window treatments).
2. Add big furniture.
3. Accessorize.

When couples blend homes, the shell doesn't usually create too much friction and, in fact, as you will see in chapter 11 where we talk about wall color as the great unifier, the right walls can integrate a merged couple's disparate furniture.

The furniture and accessories, however, are where the negotiating begins.

Invariably, regardless of how much furniture you have collectively, you will have gaps to fill, spaces in your home where neither partner's furnishings will work. Buying furniture together is a great way to invest in your look and your future. Start with something big in your combined style.

WHAT SOFA ARE YOU?

All the designers I spoke with about the topic of blending agreed: the biggest pieces in the home set the tone. And the biggest piece is often the sofa. Whichever way your sofa goes, your home will follow. This was our moment.

We both wanted a light-colored sofa, something off-white, for the great room in the new house. The sofas I had, a matched pair, were a soft blue-gray velvet. We'd earmarked them for the upstairs landing, a place to kick back and watch television. DC's black leather sofa, we agreed, was ready for another home. So we sold it on Craigslist for $100, and went sofa shopping.

DC and I had already picked out several big-ticket items together. In just the year before we got married, we'd collaborated on the purchase of a car, an engagement ring, and a house. But all of that paled in comparison to picking a sofa. You want to get to know a person, go furniture shopping together.

"I didn't think it would be so hard," I said, as we left our sixth store of the evening. DC insisted that buying a sofa was not something you do online.

"Or take so long," DC added. He was being remarkably patient as I ruminated over the many variables—back style, arms, feet, height, foam, and fill—that had never seemed important to him until now.

"I know it seems like I'm turning something that should be simple into a PhD thesis," I said, trying to justify my obsession, "but we have to think these things through; every decision about arms and legs and backs and fabric has a ripple effect."

"And here I thought that what mattered was comfort and price."

"That, too!" I said. "And lead time! Why does it take eight weeks to get a sofa?"

"Because people can't make up their minds," he said.

Over the past several days, DC and I had looked at hundreds of sofas both online and in stores. To make sure we got the size right, we'd marked a large rectangle on the great room floor with masking tape. We stared at the shape trying to manifest that ideal sofa.

Part of why this was taking so long was that this sofa, the largest statement in the largest room of our new house, would dictate the design direction of our merged households. The Ideal Sofa would be the kingpin that would hold together—or not—our eclectic blended ensemble of furniture.

"A sofa is a key player in any room," agreed Jen Sypeck, the vice-president of Home Fashion Office at Ross Stores, when I called for advice. "The sofa's style sets the stage: traditional, transitional, modern, or relaxed. Pick wrong, and you end up with one expensive mistake that just keeps giving."

Sypeck then took me through the decision tree she tells buyers to use when selecting a sofa. First, figure out function. Is the sofa going in a formal space or a heavily used area? Does it need to withstand pets and kids, or only the occasional adult conversation? Next, size up your room and decide how big you want the sofa. Tape it out; consider scale, traffic flow, and other furniture in the room. Be sure whatever you pick can get into the house, up the stairs, through the door, and into the room. Then select style. In our case, we knew that we wanted the sofa to be transitional to modernize other traditional pieces that would go in the room.

"This is where people freeze," I say. "Most don't know contemporary from classic, or retro from rustic."

So Sypeck and I came up with the following little quiz to help you figure out what sofa style best suits you:

HOW DO YOU LIKE YOUR BACK?
A. Tufted or generously padded
B. Tight and fitted
C. Loose pillows

HOW DO YOU LIKE YOUR LEGS?
A. Skirted or carved
B. Straight or tapered
C. Bun feet

HOW DO YOU LIKE YOUR ARMS?
A. Rounded
B. Square or barely there
C. Super stuffed

WHAT BEST DESCRIBES YOUR PERSONAL STYLE?

A.   I like classic, tailored, timeless appeal.

B.   The leaner, cleaner, and more minimal the look, the better it is.

C.   Comfort rules. I'd rather wear old jeans and a soft sweater than anything else.

- If you chose all or mostly **A**'s, you're a classic. Your style leans toward timeless traditional.

- If you chose **A**'s and **B**'s, you're transitional and feel at home with a mix of old and new.

- If you chose mostly **B**'s, you veer toward modern looks, a tighter, cleaner, less fussy interior.

- A lot of **C**'s indicates you like a casual cottage style, one that says relax, put your feet up, and call the dog to curl up beside you.

The Big Moment

When the day came to place our sofa order, DC and I walked into the furniture showroom and we could hear our saleswoman approaching before we saw her. Her big laugh, perfume, and the clacking of her five-inch heels preceded her by a good thirty seconds.

After two weeks of sofa shopping online and on foot, DC and I had narrowed our search down to a creamy beige contemporary 84-inch (2 m) sofa that fit our well-honed criteria: comfortable but not too casual, classic but modern, three seat cushions instead of two (so the person in the middle would not fall into the great divide), and well-made.

The saleswoman gave us each a hug, the kind shared among members of big families, though we'd only met her once. She knew the sofa we were interested in, so she squired us toward it, cutting through the store with purpose.

We followed her perfume, and I felt myself fading into obscurity with every step. I caught a glimpse of myself in a store mirror: my brown hair sprouting into a head of broccoli from the Florida humidity nicely complemented my businesslike blue dress and sensible low heels. The reflection paled in comparison to the glitzy blond saleswoman in her rhinestone-trimmed yellow dress, hair slicked back into a well-controlled bun.

We were a study in contrasts, all right, with our Ginger and MaryAnn styles. Though our styles weren't a match, she helped DC and me zero in on the best sofa for us. We learned the following sofa-buying tips:

- **MAKE IT FIT.** The most common mistake consumers make is buying a piece that may be right for their home but not their bodies. Furniture is not one size fits all. The right sofa provides lumbar support and lets your feet comfortably touch the ground. If the sofa isn't comfortable, you've missed the point. It is best if you can sit in it before you buy.

- **GO NEUTRAL.** Nine out of ten customers choose a neutral-colored sofa over a patterned one, my experts tell me. That allows the most versatility. A neutral is usually off-white, beige, taupe, or soft gray. Woven neutrals—fabrics that look solid but have color subtly woven in—make it easy to add colors and patterns. The sofa we bought looks creamy beige, but a close look reveals fine threads of rust, denim blue, brown, and charcoal.

- **CREATE YOUR BASE.** To give our great room a cohesive foundation and a neutral base to build on, we also bought a chair and ottoman in the same neutral fabric.

- **LOOK AHEAD.** When choosing between a single sofa or two, a sofa plus a chair or love seat, or a sectional, keep the long-term in mind. Sectionals are inviting to sprawl on, and can be custom fit to a space, but that's the catch. They may not transition well into your next space. If you're renting, or see yourself moving in a few years, opt for pieces that are more versatile, like an 84-inch sofa and a pair of chairs, or two love seats.

- **DON'T SKIMP.** A sofa is a staple piece in most homes. You will likely keep it for a long time, see it every day, and use it often. Invest in quality, such as frames made of hardwood (not pine), and solid construction.

LITTLE STUFF MATTERS, TOO

When blending households, the big stuff tends to get most of the attention, but at least as—if not more—important are the smaller household items you use every day. While more of my large items landed in our new house, DC's housewares beat mine hands down. And that went a long way toward making the merger feel balanced.

When we put my housewares up against his, DC's won every round: cutlery, Tupperware, cookware, casserole dishes, toasters, irons, kitchen utensils, barware, bakeware, tableware, and on, his trumped mine almost every time.

"For someone to feel at home and represented in a house," said designer Mark Brunetz, "what matters is not the size of the items they bring to the mix, but how often they're used. The pillows, the coasters, silverware, the coffee maker, those are the items we touch every day."

He *would* have to bring up the coffee maker.

DC and I shared more than a fondness for coffee. We also both had a strong attachment to our respective coffee makers. This was another negotiation that hit an impasse. I could relinquish my blender and my toaster (which my daughter happily took) in favor of his, but my coffee maker? I loved the fragrant dark brew that my machine dripped through a cone filter into a clear carafe. DC believed the coffee dispensed from his carafe-less, push-the-lever-and-fill-your-cup coffee maker was superior.

We got stuck. So . . . we kept both. For months they sat side by side on the kitchen counter of the Happy Yellow House, his and hers coffee makers, which looked as stupid as it was. Each morning I would brew my coffee in my machine, and he would make his coffee in his. This went on for an irrationally long time until my aversion to having unnecessary items on the counter overtook my desire to have my own coffee maker. That, plus the memory of whose dining room table we still had, convinced me to let my coffee maker go. And I survived.

"Are you less of a person for giving up the coffee maker?" Brunetz asked me when I confessed this tale of stubbornness.

"No," I said shamefully. (Maybe, I thought.)

"No one ever has giver-up remorse."

Dealing with Duplicates

When eliminating duplicates, handle as much as possible before the big blend. You don't want to have two barbecue grills converging at the new place.

Then haul all the multiples of each type out—all beverage glasses, clothing irons, barbecue tools, bedsheets, brooms, pasta pots, waffle irons, candlesticks—and line them up. Then ask yourself two questions:

1. *How many of this item do we need?* This question often gets bypassed when couples just want to keep everything that is still in good condition. But that's a mistake. Let's use sheets as an example. No home needs more than two sets of sheets per bed: one to "wear" and one to air. Choose the two best sets for your bed and for the other beds in the house, and let the rest go (although those in cold climates you may want to keep two flannel sets for winter per bed as well). You'll get the best of both of your collections and won't clog your linen closets with excess.

2. *Which ones are (honestly, objectively) better?* Evaluate the duplicates and determine which ones work better, are newer, and are a better brand or better quality. Put the rest in the to-go pile.

11

Color, the Great Unifier

After DC and I moved into the Happy Yellow House and cobbled together a yours, mine, and ours series of furniture compromises, the place looked all right, but it still didn't click. This would take some time to figure out and fix, we agreed. But we also recognized that we'd come a long way, and declared the place good enough *for now* (a dangerous pair of words we'll talk about later).

We decided to hit the pause button on the house and instead turn our attention to planning our wedding, a smallish affair of about fifty family members and close friends. We'd set the date for six months after the move and merger. Putting decor decisions on hold until after the wedding was a good, sensible plan, which meant, of course, we would have to mess it up.

Sure enough, just ten days before the wedding, I had the mad idea to host the rehearsal dinner (really a pre–wedding day party for loved ones coming in from afar) at our new house instead of at a restaurant.

About two dozen guests were flying in from five states. I felt having them to the house for dinner the night before the wedding would provide a warmer welcome and let us spend more time together.

"Let's have the party here," I said to DC. "It would be simpler, less expensive, and more fun for everyone."

"Won't that be a lot of trouble?" he asked.

"We'll have the barbecue restaurant cater. Easy shmeasy."

"Are you up for hosting a dinner party the day before the wedding? Won't you be having your nails done or something?"

Among the many reasons I love DC is his utter reasonableness.

"We'll be fine," I said, waving my hand as if batting a gnat. "I love to entertain."

Soon, the reality of what I had done set in. I looked around the house and saw how far from pulled together it was, and panicked. The most important people in our combined lives were about to see our home for the first time, and it wasn't ready! *I* wasn't ready!

Suddenly, I was frantically scurrying around like Lucille Ball on roller skates with her hair on fire. I texted my best friend, Susan Beane, who lives halfway across the country and who confers with me on all matters of home design: "I have a design job for you. We need to find an accent rug to go under the glass cocktail table in the great room."

She and I had previously agreed that whatever went under this glass table would inspire the design direction for the whole house. It was a centerpiece, and it had to be something DC and I both loved.

Within minutes, she was peppering me with links to rugs, which I shared with DC. Together we responded: "Too gray." "Too ethnic." "Too busy."

Some I liked, but he didn't. And some went the other way around.

She kept pushing for one peacock-motif rug, which featured a textured blend of blues, greens, and touches of ochre on a cream background. It was pretty, but DC and I kept rejecting it because, though we liked it, we couldn't see it in our home.

"It's too obvious," I said. "I'm picturing something subtler."

"You want a statement," she said.

"We don't have any deep blue or green in our home."

"The rug speaks to me."

"It speaks to me, too," I said. "It says, 'I don't fit in your home!'"

"Try it."

The rug arrived two days later. I put it under the coffee table where it was so loud, I had to step outside into the courtyard. DC put it this way, "It's about as subtle as an Iron Maiden concert."

I texted pictures to Susan.

"Okay." She was on the phone in seconds. "The rug is gorgeous."

"We love the rug, but it doesn't go."

"Make it go."

"It upstages the whole house."

"What's to upstage? You haven't decorated." Best friends can say what no one else can.

She was right. We had furnished the house, but we hadn't decorated it. We had to start somewhere. I huddled with DC. We agreed that this rug was beautiful but would be a commitment piece. However, if we kept it, we could work in some colorful modern art he'd been eyeing, and I could finally have an inspiration piece to run with. Plus, it was as neutral as Switzerland in the sense that it didn't come from his place or mine.

I called Susan. "We'd like to make it work, but it will take a lot to tie it in—pillows, art, accessories."

"So?"

"In case you forgot, I'm getting married in a week. I can't pull this off in time."

"Why not?" Her voice sagged with disappointment.

"Okay," I said. "What do we need to do?"

Next minute, I was in a frenzy looking through DC's and my joint collection of accessories for blue and green throw pillows and accents, trying to make this rug, which had taken on the life of a family pet, belong.

Two days later, I was on the phone with Susan. "I am giving up," I said. "It isn't working. The rug's going back. I can't make the colors work." She was quiet, as if I'd just told her I were dying or something.

Then, just as I was about to roll up the rug for good, I had a thought so scary I almost couldn't say it. "I have an idea," I whispered. "What if I painted the dining room next door a deep sea blue to balance out the rug."

"Oooooo," she said.

I was afraid of that. My already high levels of adrenaline tripled. I torpedoed to the paint store, bringing home two dozen paint swatches: a handful of dark blues for the dining room, and a selection of other colors for the rest of the house. I put them all up against that instigator rug. Then I superhumanly compressed a two-week color-selecting process into ten minutes, and called Bob, our painter, who, being a married man, grasped the importance of this absurd situation. He picked up on my derangement and rearranged his schedule to start painting the next day.

With five days before the wedding, he painted the dining room Sherwin-Williams Bunglehouse Blue. Meanwhile, DC and I culled a collection of paint colors for the rest of the house—Colonial Yellow, Sage, Dutch-Tile Blue, and Chrysanthemum (a dusty terra-cotta)—all colors that belong to the Sherwin-Williams Historic Collection. All the colors went with each other and with the kingpin rug. Bob and his partner painted the whole house inside, all in time for the wedding, and all because of Susan, which proves what I often say: a task will expand to fill the amount of time you have.

Amazingly, the palette, anchored by the rug, and the courageous blue in the dining room, pulled together the whole house—despite its array of furniture styles. Just like that, the house clicked. I sent pictures to Susan, who called it "a stroke of genius."

"You'd better say that," I said.

On the eve of our wedding, thanks in part to the magic of color but also to the magic of love, our Happy Yellow House looked and felt like a place ready to celebrate.

THE SECRET TO INSPIRED COLOR

Many couples I interviewed who had blended their homes had this in common: They had bought a piece of art or an area rug that they both loved together. What they didn't always realize was that they had their starting point in hand.

More than any other design choice, color sets the mood and emotion of a home. The colors you paint your walls—or choose for accent pillows, wall art, and area rugs—not only define the tone, but also can either unify a home or make it feel disconnected.

Thankfully, color is also the easiest design variable to change. Most of the big pieces in a home—the hutches, dressers, chests, bookcases, and the bedroom and dining room sets, furniture those in the business call case goods—are typically wood, and often fairly neutral in color.

Once you decide whose case goods you're keeping, even if you're dealing with your Scandinavian bookcase and your partner's walnut desk, a sure color palette can bridge the style mix and serve as the great galvanizer, a decor bridge. And, as we've illustrated, that unifying palette should come from a piece you both love.

Finding an inspiration piece is a design principle I have followed for years. When choosing a color palette for your home, start with a painting, rug, fabric, or wallpaper swatch, and let the colors in that piece be your dowsing rod. This advice is especially helpful when merging households.

Years later, while talking with interior designer Sue Wadden, director of color marketing for Sherwin-Williams, I learned why this principle works so well.

I was telling Wadden the story of how DC and I relied on an area rug to divine the colors in our new home. "Using a great piece of art, area rug, or fabric that contains colors you love as a guide is foolproof because the colors have been curated," she said.

That was it! *Curated* is the secret word. Trained artists select and combine—*or curate*—the colors used in these beautiful pieces, which is why the colors work. Lightbulbs went off. The stars aligned. The Rubik's cube clicked into place, and I understood.

My epiphany was this: Artists are to color choice what surgeons are to surgery. You wouldn't remove your own appendix, would you? Artists who curate the colors that go in rugs, textiles, wallpaper, or, heck, even giftwrap, have color training. That expertise helps them know what combinations go together and, more important, which ones don't.

How hard is that? you ask. After all, you got a sixty-four pack of crayons as a kid. You know your primary from your secondary colors. Well, I'll tell you, color is complicated. I learned how complicated years ago when I took a color theory class at UCLA and studied not only pigment and hue, but also value and tone, and undertone, and tetrads and triads. I learned that yellow can be cool, and blue can be warm; that neutrals can be accent colors, and accent colors can be neutrals.

I learned enough to know that certain folks know a lot more than I do about color, and that their expertise is worth latching on to.

So here's where I'm going with this. When choosing a color palette for your home, let the experts give you a running start. Don't try to cobble the combination together yourself. Rely on colors already curated. In other words, when putting together a palette, let experts lead the way.

Painting companies have also made color selection easier by vetting colors and combining them into families. So you can confidently pick from one color family and know that the curated colors—even those as different as teal, mocha, and persimmon—will get along.

"I always recommend people stay on one color strip and move up and down it when choosing wall colors for their homes," I told Wadden, as we talked about choosing interior wall color. "Then I go and paint my walls five colors."

I sent her some pictures to show her what I was talking about. "Nicely done!" she said, to my great relief.

"You don't think the dining room is too bold?"

"Bunglehouse Blue is one of my all-time favorite colors," she said. "You are definitely taking a risk when you go with a deep color, but when it works, like it does here, the payoff is so much more rewarding."

As for the rest of the house, she added, "I love the idea of painting rooms different colors, so long as there is an intentional palette. Sure, a beautiful and elegant way to design your home is to stay on one strip. You will get a really sure, safe look. Going off the strip and incorporating different colors is more difficult, but you pulled it off because you started with something you loved, the rug, and paired that with a vetted color collection."

In this case, by going with the curated colors in the rug DC and I both agreed on paired with wall colors in the also-curated Historic Collection, we let the experts lead the color way and got a great unifying look, one that beautifully bridged our eclectic blend of furniture in a way that said *yours*, *mine*, and *ours*.

Cultivating Color

A carefully selected color palette is not only fun to find with your partner, but it is also a great unifier and can be the decor bridge that gives merged houses the cohesive look couples crave. Here, two of my favorite designers, Sue Wadden and Betty Lou Phillips, offer their suggestions for working with color:

- **FIND INSPIRATION.** Couples working to create a home together can't go wrong by starting with something they both love and making color connections from there, says Wadden. "Find a fabric, pillow, piece of art, or rug that already has curated color in it and let it inspire your blended home's palette."
- **USE PAINTS FROM ONE FAMILY.** Once you have a palette, says Wadden, help your home cohere either by painting

rooms inside your house from colors on the same strip, or by using different colors from the same collection, which most paint companies have vetted into groupings of colors that work together. (For instance, Home Depot's BEHR® paint line has several curated palettes: Artisan, Cottage, Classic, Modern, and Neutral. Each contains twenty-eight colors that all get along.) This will give your home a unified feel.

- **LOOK OUTSIDE.** Nature is a natural curator of color. Look to her for background and accent colors, says Dallas interior designer Betty Lou Phillips, author of *The French Way with Design* (2014) and many more design books. "Be open to seeing what you like together, and then pick up and follow the clues."

- **WATCH THE PROPORTIONS.** To achieve color harmony, you also need to mix colors in the right proportions, Phillips explains. This is another way an artist's eye is helpful. Those trained in working with color can identify which colors to combine and how much of each. "The music is in the fabric. Look to the composition for how the colors are mixed and in what proportions. Add and subtract until you achieve balance."

- **NOTE COLOR PLACEMENT.** "Position is as important as proportion," Phillips says. "You don't want a color that sticks out because it doesn't relate to the rest of the room." If your accent is orange, for instance, and you have an orange stripe in a seat cushion, place an orange candle across the room, an orange flower somewhere else. "Distribute the color in some way, even a small way."

- **READ BETWEEN THE LABEL LINES.** The designers behind the scenes at paint companies also name colors intentionally, Phillips notes. "The name of a paint offers hints to its best context. Davenport Tan [Benjamin Moore] is a traditional classic. Procession Pink [Ralph Lauren] strikes a nice note for a girl's room."

- **CONSIDER YOUR TRIM**. Stronger colors work best against a light trim, says Wadden. In my case, the dining room's deep blue was against white wainscoting and plantation shutters. If you have dark trim and dark furniture, go lighter on the walls. Darker colors also work better in rooms with a lot of natural light. Avoid dark colors in windowless rooms.

- **CHECK THE MAP**. In general, the closer you live to the equator, the bolder you can be with color. In Florida, we can be brighter and are at home with more lively color. Closer to the North Pole, colors get more muted, veering toward beige, taupe, and gray. Think Hawaiian hibiscus and Boston tweed, offers Wadden.

Now, find your color way and go!

12

Make a Great Upholsterer Part of Your Transition Team

My two armchairs were on their way to the island of orphaned furniture. This gave me a little bit of a sick feeling. I tried to be clearheaded as I edited which furniture from my house and DC's would make the cut in our new blended home. Many items landed on the exit ramp, which felt healthy and right, like a vegetable-juice cleanse.

But I was having a hard time parting with the chairs. I liked them. They were well-made, in good condition, and solidly comfortable. The only sin they had committed was that they no longer went with the updated vision for our new home.

DC and I had agreed on a transitional interior for the Happy Yellow House, a tricky decor style that bridges traditional with contemporary (see pages 84–85). Some traditional items, just like people, move forward better than others. And when seen in the light of our new future, these gold-and-blue upholstered chairs looked, well—I had to be honest—fusty.

Their overtly traditional lines and old-world fabric looked passé. So the chairs sat in my garage awaiting the next truck from the Sharing Center to come by. And that nagged at me. I developed an irrational identification with those chairs, and thought, "I know how I would feel if someone showed me the exit door just because I didn't fit in."

Maybe it's my Scottish heritage, but I am frugal at my core. I'm philosophically opposed to replacing something that's inherently good with something likely to be inferior—even if it is more stylish. I believe in reusing, repurposing, and rehabilitating when possible in taking care of what's mine, not just ejecting it for a newer model, tempting though that may be.

So, I took my own advice.

"I thought we were getting rid of those," DC said when he saw the chairs back in the house with swatches of contemporary fabric samples spread out on them.

"I was thinking, maybe we could re-cover and not replace them." I said.

"I thought you said they wouldn't work."

"I changed my mind," I said, exercising my female prerogative. "I mean, we can discuss it, but putting contemporary fabric on a traditional chair is the ultimate transitional statement." I hoped I sounded convincing, because I was still teetering, and really wanted the chairs to win.

"Is it worth it?"

"We'll see."

DC adjusted his eyebrows, which had been in a perpetually raised state since we started the whole process.

I contacted Dean Stills, co-owner of Stills Upholstery, a family business in Longwood, Florida, which has been resurrecting and transforming furniture for four decades.

"We live in such a throwaway society," he said. "People give away a high-quality sofa that their grandparents paid $3,500 for in 1975, and buy something that isn't real wood . . . because they think it's cooler." As Stills and I talked, I felt better about re-covering and not replacing these good old chairs. I found a contemporary fabric that DC liked, and that, he agreed, would salvage the chairs in his mind, and serve as a bridge for them to work in our new home. And we saved them.

RE-COVER OR REPLACE?
WHAT TO DO WITH TIRED FURNITURE

Stills took me through all the considerations folks should keep in mind before showing a piece of upholstered furniture the door.

- QUALITY. "Not every piece is worth re-covering," Stills told me. Much depends on the quality of the frame, and the piece's condition. "If it's a cheap piece, throw it away and start over. If you aren't sure how well made a piece is, pick it up. Heavier usually means better made. If it's a sofa, and the frame bows or bends when you pick up a corner, it's low end. Also, sit in the seat and scooch. If it's rickety, it's not well made. Better-made pieces feel stable, and are made of hard wood like oak, ash, or maple, not soft material like pine, plastic, or composite. Pieces put together with doweled joints hold up better than butted joints. Also, note age. In this case, older is better. Anything made before 1985 usually has a high-end wooden frame. Wood gets harder as it gets older."

- **CONNECTION.** Do you have a family attachment to the piece? If Grandma's sofa or the chair you sat in with Dad isn't a decorative fit anymore or it's worn, new upholstery can give it a new life for another generation.

- **COMFORT.** If it's a favorite chair, and no other chair feels quite like it, it might be worth a chairlift.

- **COST.** If a piece was expensive, re-covering it will be cheaper than replacing it with something equally well made. Reupholstering is often 50 to 60 percent of the cost of replacing, Stills explained. My armchairs would cost around $800 to $1,000 each to replace. Re-covering cost $500 per chair ($320 for labor, $180 for fabric).

- **CONFIGURATION.** If the lines are good and the item is integral to your decor, and only the color or fabric pattern are wrong, re-cover.

- **CUSTOMIZATION.** If you like choice, you will have many more fabrics to choose from if you reupholster than if you buy a chair from a furniture store, which will offer a limited fabric selection. Reupholstering lets you choose and mix fabrics to customize pieces to fit your decor.

- **CONVENIENCE**. Shopping for new furniture is time-consuming. If you have a piece you know works but that needs a refresh, re-covering lets you avoid the hassle of starting from scratch.
- **CONSCIENCE**. Repurposing just feels better than replacing, and is better for the planet.
- **COMPROMISE**. If one half of the couple loves the piece but the other half doesn't, re-covering it can please both parties.

WHEN FURNITURE DOESN'T FIT, THINK OUTSIDE THE BOX

On paper, my two smoky-blue, faux-suede sofas fit beautifully on the upstairs landing of the Happy Yellow House. DC agreed. I had drawn them on my to-scale floor plan. (Remember that?) There, the two 7-foot (2 m) matched sofas met at a tidy right angle and nested comfortably in the corner. A coffee table sat nearby. One sofa was positioned along the shorter part of the angle, the half wall, which was 8½ feet (2.6 m) long; the other sofa was placed against the adjoining longer wall.

The arrangement offered a perfect view of the articulating flat screen in the opposite corner, forming a cozy TV and game area. I could already smell the popcorn and sense the Scrabble® victories.

As soon as the movers set the sofas down, I discovered my mistake, which reminded me again how lucky it is for the world that I do not do rocket surgery. I had thought an 8½-foot wall would be long enough for a 7-foot sofa. But I failed to allow for the *depth* of the sofas. They were each 3-feet deep. The back corners of these sofas didn't need to meet; their *front* corners did. When they did, a hollow formed in the adjoining corner that ate up 3 feet of wall one way and 3 feet the other. And so, the 7-foot sofa on the 8½-foot wall jutted past the end of the wall and into the hallway by 18 inches. *Sigh.*

In any case—and those of you who saw this coming can just go away now and study your differential equations—all you have to know is now the sofa on the half wall stuck out beyond the wall awkwardly, like that kid with the growth spurt at the seventh-grade dance.

No matter how hard I pushed and squeezed and wished it weren't so, the sofa simply—like Cinderella's shoe on her ugly stepsister's foot—did not fit. This not only looked ridiculous but was also a hazard for anyone coming around the corner at the top of the stairs. Just when you thought it was safe to turn where the wall ends, wham! You're hit by a defensive linebacker wearing blue faux suede. I mulled my options:

- **LIVE WITH IT?** No. That would grate.
- **REARRANGE THE SOFAS TO FACE EACH OTHER?** That would defeat the purpose of a corner seating area to watch movies.
- **ELIMINATE ONE SOFA?** That would hurt. And I liked the sofas, especially together. Plus, I wanted the extra seating.

- **REPLACE ONE SOFA WITH A SMALLER ONE?** Forget about it. I wouldn't be able to match the existing sofa, and two mismatched sofas would look like one of those college lounges outfitted with parental castoffs and flea market finds.

- **REPLACE ONE SOFA WITH TWO CHAIRS?** That seating arrangement would feel too formal for a room meant for kicking back and watching movies.

- **GET RID OF BOTH SOFAS, AND START OVER? OUCH.** The thought of losing one sofa was bad enough. Scrapping two and buying two more or a sectional felt doubly painful and expensive.

As I continued to consider these sorry options, I kept thinking, "If I could only chop off one end . . ."

Then it hit me. "And why not?" I grabbed my phone and looked up the question "Can you shorten a sofa?"

Yes, you can! I called Stills, who said, "We shorten sofas all the time."

"Really? Is it worth it?"

"If it's a good sofa, shortening it is definitely cheaper than buying a new one," he said. Or in my case, buying two new ones.

The next day, he picked up one sofa and took it to his shop, where it underwent sofa surgery. His crew cut out the middle section and smooshed (that's the technical term) the two ends together like bookends, turning the three-cushioned sofa into a two-cushion love seat. Magically, the back panel of fabric stayed in one piece, no seam.

Three days later, the sofa was back home, reminding me of those before and after pictures in a miracle weight-loss ad: same person, one-third smaller. The cost: $550—a lot less than a new sofa and a whole lot less than two.

"Yours was the perfect situation," said Stills. "The sofa was in great shape, well made, with a solid hard-oak frame and double-dowel Dutch stretchers, and fit your decor."

And now it fits the space, too.

Upholstery Magic

Amazed, I asked what other tricks—besides straight up re-covering furniture with new fabric—good upholsterers could do that we home blenders and our furniture might benefit from. These were some of the suggestions:

- **ADJUST TO FIT**. Besides making a sofa shorter, a good upholsterer can make one longer. (Sofas with externally visible wood frames not covered by fabric aren't good candidates for either revision.) They can also make a traditional sofa more modern and vice versa, by making round arms square and square arms round, or by straightening out an arched back and curving a straight one. "I've had customers look at the piece when we're done and say, 'That's not my sofa,'" Stills said.

- **CHANGE THE STYLE**. An upholsterer can also make contemporary pieces look more traditional and traditional pieces more contemporary. Adding topstitching, for instance, makes a piece look more modern, Stills told me. Adding a skirt, fringe, buttons, or welts will make it more traditional. Removing buttons and tufting makes it more contemporary, as does narrowing an overstuffed arm.

- **ADD REINFORCEMENT.** For larger customers, an upholsterer can add padding and reinforce frames, so sofas and chairs hold up better and sit comfortably.

13

When Art Tastes Collide

Walls painted? Check. Major furniture in place? Check. We're still speaking to each other. Good. Because the third stage in every interior design project, and the hardest part for merging households, lay ahead—adding art and accessories that tell both partners' stories.

This is where personalities get snuffed or showcased, and where the goal should be displaying pieces that reflect your past lives (not ex-wives), that acknowledge the kids evenly, and that feature a delicate dance of the two of you to this point and going forward.

In short, this is where you tell your story—only, beautifully edited.

DC AND I HAD NEGOTIATED THROUGH the major landmines—we thought. We'd merged (and acquired) furnishings together, and thought the worst was over. However, all that paled in comparison to our disagreements over art.

He likes shiny metal. I like antiqued wood. He likes bold. I like subtle. While DC and I both *claimed* to like a wide variety of art, in fact, we both had a stubborn little knot tied around what we thought should hang in our home.

"I do like a lot of art, but I don't consider that art," is a snippet from one exchange on the subject. I won't say who said it, but it was the less diplomatic one.

I lean toward traditional landscapes and colorful abstracts. DC likes hyper-realistic art—the kind that looks as if you could lift the chocolate from the box—and also fiery-looking mixed-media art blazed onto aluminum. (One of his favorite artists literally got his start painting the gas tanks of motorcycles; not kidding.)

All this might not have mattered were it not for a large— 10-foot high by 20-foot long (3 × 6 m)—wall in the great room of our Happy Yellow House. The wall stood empty for months after we moved in as we debated what to hang on it. We held out hope to have it dressed before the wedding guests arrived, but that was looking doubtful.

We couldn't imagine finding one large statement piece that we both would like enough to make the focal point of this most public room. So I began envisioning a gallery wall, an eclectic mix of his taste and mine, of traditional and modern art, photos past and present; an art concert, like fusion jazz. (I can tell you're snickering, but have some faith, please.)

I reached out for some help from an expert neutral party. "Choosing art can be one of the most contentious parts of a relationship for couples," said Alex Farkas, cofounder of UGallery.com, when I told him about my dilemma.

"Your vision of a gallery wall is such a great solution for you two," he said.

"It's not a copout?"

"You both have already lived different lives. This wall can tell the story of your coming together."

"In a head-on collision," I said, smacking my knuckles together. "Where do we even start?"

"In the middle," Farkas said, more politician than gallery owner. "Work together to pick one main piece you both feel strongly about."

"Oh, we find lots of those," I said. "I feel strongly one way. He feels strongly the other."

"Make that the centerpiece, then build what you each like around that. It's okay if it's not homogenous."

"Oh, don't worry. It won't be."

BUILDING A GALLERY WALL

Though, in theory, a gallery wall expressing two individuals coming together could be the perfect marriage of their art, passions, and lives, if not done carefully, this collaborative approach could end up looking like a middle-school welcome wall on back-to-school night. To build an aesthetically pleasing gallery wall, Farkas offers these tips:

- **GATHER THE POSSIBILITIES.** Start with your centerpiece art, and then pull together candidates that could work around it and tell your story. Don't worry about the frames just yet. In addition to artwork, mix in photos past and present, Farkas says. Perhaps add a shelf and put decorative items on it.

- **IF YOU'RE MIXING, GO ALL IN.** A bunch of too-similar paintings together gets boring, but contrasting pieces enhance one another. "There is no hard and fast rule about what you can and can't combine," Farkas notes. "What holds it all together is your story."

- **LET FRAMES BUILD BRIDGES.** Framing is a great way to unify art, but don't use the same frame for everything. That too can get boring. To bridge old and new, put contemporary frames on traditional art and vice versa. "Big ornate classical frames on contemporary abstract art are very hip," he says. Mix in some frameless pieces on stretched canvas, too.

- **COMPOSE ON THE FLOOR.** Before you pound holes in your wall, lay out your composition on the floor. Move items around, and add and remove until you get good proportions. You don't need to achieve symmetry, but you should have balance. Avoid trapped or pinched space. Trapped space is when an area of blank wall gets bordered on four sides. Pinched space occurs when art is too close together, or too close to the edge of a window or a corner. Make margins about the same.

- **HANG IT RIGHT.** Typically, art should hang so the middle of the piece is 60 inches (1.5 m) from the floor, but on a gallery wall, pieces can hang higher and lower, Farkas says. Just don't hang art so high you can't see it, or so low it touches your knees.

- **CONSIDER THE REST OF THE ROOM.** A busy gallery wall will command a lot of visual attention, so make sure the furnishings in the rest of the room don't offer too much competition.

- **BUY PRETTY BUT PRACTICAL.** Art sellers tend to say, "Anything goes. If you love it, buy it." But practicality is a factor. "Art should look good with your furnishings, too," Farkas advises.
- **TASTES EVOLVE.** "The more art you look at, the more your tastes change," Farkas says, giving me hope that as DC and I take our creative journey together, we will learn to like new styles of art together.

Full disclosure: Though DC and I came close to creating a gallery wall, and even had one mapped out, we did not ultimately move forward with it because the unthinkable happened. We found one big picture, we both (sort of) agreed on. Farkas liked that idea, too.

"Besides a gallery wall, another way to fill a big wall is to go with one large statement piece," he said. "That can be spectacular."

The trick, of course, is finding that one piece that represents a marriage of minds.

MIX IT UP—BUT BEAUTIFULLY

To make sure I hadn't sold out completely, I called a friend, interior designer Elaine Griffin, for some reassurance. When I asked if I could mix traditional oils and modern abstracts on metal in the same house, she'd screamed, "YES! Not only can you mix, you should! The chicest interiors combine both." Here are some more tips from Griffin on mixing art styles that home blenders can use:

- **SET SOME GROUND RULES**. "First of all," she says, "remember, part of being a couple means compromise." However, while both partners can bring to the table what they like, each also has veto power. But use the privilege sparingly.

- **CHECK THE OTHER BOXES FIRST**. Before you get to "Whose is it?" and "Do I like it?"—you need to first satisfy a few other items on the art checklist: scale, color, and subject matter. First, the art must relate to the wall it's on and the room it's in. Small pieces work best in small spaces and large artworks need large walls where viewers can appreciate them at a distance. Once you nail down the size, focus on the color and subject matter. "A blown-up photo of Muhammad Ali doesn't go in the kitchen. That's for the man cave," Griffin says. If the scale, color, and subject matter work, the art will, too, regardless of style.

- **UNDERSTAND COLLECTOR VS. DECORATOR**. Art buyers come from two perspectives, Griffin notes. Collectors buy what they love, regardless of where or whether it will be displayed. (That's DC). Decorators pick art because it works in a space. (That's me.) "The two approaches are not mutually exclusive," she said. "You did both. You approached the choice from a design perspective. You knew what size you wanted, and what color. Then you worked to find one that fit your criteria from an artist your husband wanted to collect." Score!

- **USE FRAMES TO UNIFY**. "Similar frames can tie dissimilar pieces together, even if the style of the art is different," she advises. "Framing is the secret to making opposites attract." Similar subject matter in different styles can also connect. "A modern landscape next to an old landscape, that to me is chic," Griffin adds.

- **CONSULT THE NEIGHBORHOOD COUNCIL.** Still can't agree? Ask family, friends, and neighbors to weigh in, but explain to them beforehand that you want an honest opinion, and not to throw their vote, she says.

"At the end of the day, what matters is the relationship between pieces," Griffin told me, "not how similar they are. Different is better."

Which is true for couples, too, apparently.

THE ART OF NEGOTIATING ART

Besides having different tastes in art, DC and I come to art from philosophically different places. (Neither approach is wrong, mind you, but I am more right.) DC likes to collect works from known artists who have strong followings and whose pieces sell in multiple galleries. Although originals are best, he will also buy signed, numbered, or hand-embellished prints. I like to support little-known artists whose work I find at local art fairs, where I often meet the artist and take home something original.

So when DC first showed me the work of one of his favorite painters, a successful mixed-media artist who spray-paints on metal along with what looked like airbrushing to me, I laughed, which was the politest response at my disposal. But inside I was thinking, "No way!"

"It's not airbrush," DC corrected. "He uses fire and paint and grinders, and it's awesome."

"It looks like a mash-up of a rocket launch and a school of jellyfish," I said.

"He got inspired while painting the gas tanks of motorcycles," DC added.

"That does not endear me," I said.

What DC did not point out is that, since we blended our furnishings, my art dominates the vertical real estate in our home at a ratio of, oh, about my five pieces to his one. This was not lost on me. I needed to bend, and yet I felt about as flexible as a wishbone three weeks after Thanksgiving.

But then—and this is where love comes in—I remembered the dining room table, and I softened.

The thaw started with the colorful rug. Remember the blue, green, and ocher patterned rug, the one that tripped the frenzy of painting just days before the wedding? That rug?

Well, what ultimately sold DC on the rug was when I told him how we would let it inform our art and accessories. We'd need to add some strong color in pillows, wall paint, and art, I'd said, and then I'd blurted out the immortal words: "I could even see a piece by your favorite painter."

DC had launched into a series of fist pumps, as if the Steelers had just won the Super Bowl.

Like horses out of the barn, these words were not coming back.

"But it would have to be the right colors," I'd added, before this got out of control.

He did not care. He was getting his painting.

Soon after, we were standing in the artist's gallery in Scottsdale, Arizona. DC wore a 500-watt smile. And we found it. The six-panel statement piece in the right size for the great big wall, with the right colors.

And, you know what? It looked pretty great.

Eventually, our home evolved to reflect both of our tastes in art, just not always in the same room. Depending on what our respective pieces of art lent themselves to, we each claimed different rooms. My landscape oils went in the dining room and entry, where the decor was a bit more formal. He got a second piece by the mixed-media artist he likes and they both hang in the family room, which has an edgier vibe. His African artwork of animals in the wild looked at home over the leather sofa in his man cave. My prints of France grace my office. Together, we've collected more work by an Israeli artist he introduced me to, whom I also like. His work, which often features subjects dining, cheers up our kitchen and eating area. The artwork throughout our home is varied and eclectic, traditional and modern, abstract and exact, and it's us.

The art of compromise. It's a beautiful thing.

14

Accessorizing Shelves to Blend

As a writer and home designer, I am terrified by two tyrannies: the blank page and the blank wall, both of which I am obliged to fill with style and purpose. It can be daunting.

If you want to experience full-body paralysis, stand in front of an empty wall or a vacant set of built-in shelves, and attempt to decorate and accessorize them.

Under normal circumstances, this is hard enough. The petrifying forces include the fact that open shelves are basically a shout out that says: *This is my soul in 3-D. It's my taste and life on display.* And now you're doing that times two, with stuff that doesn't yet know each other.

Ideally, what is on display should represent those who live in the home—their characters, histories, interests, tastes, and travels—without coming across like a stuffy old piece of taxidermy or an illustrated *Who's Who*. That's pressure.

On top of that, in a shared space, display shelves should beautifully blend the diverse backgrounds of both partners: Her French faience. His framed fishing flies. Items must be meaningful and look good together. To create a pleasing composition, you must factor in texture, shape, color, scale, empty space, and overall balance.

All this hit me when I faced off with the built-in shelving unit in our new great room. I blended artifacts from DC's life and mine, added the most handsome books from our combined libraries, and ended up with a look that, while politically correct, still missed the mark by my lights.

I wasn't giving up.

So when I heard that shelf styling was a specialty of interior designer Jaclyn Joslin's, owner of the Kansas City home furnishings store Coveted Home, I called her for some advice.

"I see two extremes," Joslin said of the clients who call upon her to help them dress their shelves. "I either see completely empty shelves because the owners don't know what to do, or shelves stuffed with stuff."

We are in favor of the happy, well-edited medium.

SOULS ON DISPLAY

"Creating a harmonious shelf composition is tricky, even for those trained in design," admitted Joslin, which made me feel better. She offers this advice:

- CLEAR THE SLATE. Start with nothing on the shelves.
- BRING OUT THE POSSIBILITIES. Open your cabinets and haul out all shelf decor candidates, even the most unlikely, Joslin says. Together with your partner, gather

books, pretty dishes, vases, rusty old cameras, glass art, metalwork, candlesticks, clocks, potted plants, woven baskets, small framed art, and anything that appeals to you both, and set them on a table to "shop" from. Evaluate items for their sculptural qualities, color, texture, and shape, as well as for what they mean to you. (Those Native American dolls may have found their moment.)

- **PLAY**. Start with a few hardback books; add a colorful ceramic vase, then a vibrant piece of glass. Put small beside large. Tuck in a plant. Let each shelf be its own landscape, then work to be sure shelves altogether have balance.

- **ADD LAYERS**. Prop or hang art on the back wall to add depth. It's okay to place books or small accessories in front.

- **MIX MATERIALS**. When selecting finalists, aim for varying textures: ceramics, metal, wood, glass, books, textiles, plants, and artwork.

- **LEAVE PLENTY OF OPEN SPACE**. The eye needs relief. Keep adding and removing until you like the arrangement. Come back later and play some more until the shelves click.

- **PUT IN THE EFFORT**. Make collecting beautiful accessories a part of your life, Joslin says, not only when you travel, but even—and especially—when you're out shopping in your own town. Celebrate the local artists' work. "The biggest mistake I see is when people run to one store and buy a bunch of cheap accessories to fill a space." The result looks soulless. "Better to sit with a few blank spaces and wait for the right item."

- **GO EASY ON THE PHOTOS**. The second biggest mistake Joslin sees are too many framed photos. A few are okay, but too many homes have shelves crammed with pictures, which eliminates any hope of creating an edited, restrained, elegant shelf display.

- **PUT OUT YOUR BEST BOOKS.** Hardbacks look best, and a few cherished tattered ones can add character. Display books both vertically and horizontally for variety, and incorporate handsome bookends to avoid the wall-to-wall book look (although in certain rooms, like a library or office, a solid wall of books looks great).

- **EVOLVE.** Don't stop when you're done. Let the space work as a living museum. Add new items and let go of others. "Don't feel obligated to cling to what you once bought if you don't really like it anymore," Joslin says, summing up. "Move on."

15

What's in a Name?

When DC and I got married, I decided, having proven whatever I needed to prove by not changing my maiden name in my previous marriage, to take his last name. Though I continue to use my maiden name professionally on my books and columns, personally and legally I became Marni Jameson Carey. I've had monogram fever ever since.

I've tattooed many items in our home with monograms or, more exactly, duograms: our bed linens, bath towels, glassware, stationery. And I'm not done.

"Aren't they a little pretentious?" DC asked, when my monogram mania began.

"Not at all," I shot back. "A monogram elevates any item instantly. It makes the common personal, the pedestrian unique."

"I thought it just made it more expensive," he said, though I could tell he thought it was cool.

MONOGRAM AS MONIKER

When incorporated into a blended home, monograms become powerful unifying symbols. They can work like a logo, branding the relationship. When a couple or family comes under one banner, a shared name is a wonderful bond, and monograms can help celebrate and display that throughout the home.

According to the experts, a monogram can be one, two, or three letters. Technically, a monogram is for an individual, a duogram reflects a couple, and a single letter can represent a family surname.

Whether on apparel or on items throughout a home, monograms are classy, timeless, and decorative, said Kimberly Schlegel Whitman, author of *Monograms for the Home* (2015), when I called her to talk about all things monogrammed.

"I've always loved monograms," said Whitman, who is also a Dallas-based editor-at-large for *Southern Living* magazine. "I love how a single mark personalizes an item and blends a person or family with the history of a piece."

"And how they make anything look more elegant," I oozed, "like you've just added a strand of pearls."

Monograms weren't always for decoration. In ancient Rome, rulers put them on coins, and in the Middle Ages, artisans and printers used monograms to identify their work. Embroidering monograms on fabric for use in the home began to gain popularity in the eighteenth century. Today, part of the attraction of monogramming is that you can take something mass produced and ordinary, and make it uniquely yours. Or, you can use it to create a banner for your new life and identity as a couple, while personalizing your blended home.

"The top monogrammed items in the home are towels, table linens, bedding, and stationery," she said, but monograms are also popping up on less precious items like coffee mugs.

As an anniversary present, I recently bought matching his-and-hers robes for DC and myself. I had the initials *MC* put on mine and *DC* put on his. It's just one more way to say, "We're in this together."

MAKING YOUR MARK

Whether on fine linen or silver, or on bathroom towels or doormats, a distinctive monogram or duogram adds a touch of personality, class, and elegance. The tradition is as strong as ever, according to Whitman, who offers these how's and where's for placing your distinctive mark in your new blended home.

How to Make Your Mark

- **LETTER ARRANGEMENT**. If the monogram style you want features a large central initial, the surname initial goes in the middle; so, for me that would be MCJ. If the letters are all the same size, put letters in order: MJC. A duogram is a mark that incorporates the combined names of a married couple. Traditionally, the surname initial of the groom goes in the center between the initials of the partners' first names, with the woman's initial first, and the man's last, so MCD. Today, with a wide range of types of romantic partnerships, couples often just use their first name initials separated by an ampersand.

- **FONT CHOICE.** Where the item is going and what it is dictate font choice. For instance, an ornate silver tray suggests a delicate scroll, while a modern acrylic tray in a teen's room calls for block type. When choosing your font, look at your initials to see how the letters look together. Play with the order. Whitman's husband's initials, JJW, look beautiful and symmetrical when the last initial is large and central. Get a proof before you commit. Scale is important, and the trend is to go bigger, Whitman says. "Look to the person doing the monogram to guide you."

- **UNFORTUNATE COMBINATIONS.** If your initials or your duogram spell an undesirable word like PIG, switch up the sequence or go for a two-letter monogram with your partner's and your own first initials, Whitman suggests.

- **DO MAKE IT LEGIBLE.** If you can't read the letters, you've missed the point.

- **BY HAND OR MACHINE.** To find someone who does custom monogramming, ask your local tailor for a source or look online. Stores that sell wedding gifts often have suggestions. Most monograms today are done by machine, but some are still done by hand. Both are lovely, Whitman says. Machine work is more perfect, but a beautifully hand-stitched monogram on a handkerchief is nothing to sneeze at.

Where to Make Your Mark

- **THE ENTRY**. Starting at the front door, a welcome mat with the initial of the family surname, or with a duogram, makes a great opening statement.

- **THE DINING ROOM**. Silver service, table linens, and dishware have long been bearers of the family logo. Old tradition dictated that linens and serving pieces carry the monogram of the lady of the house, while the man's monogram emblazons the barware. "Today we are seeing a movement away from those old-school rules," Whitman says. Now duograms are on the rise, gracing both table and barware.

- **THE BATH**. Individual monograms on bath towels inject personality, and can also help the sorting process on wash day. Use a lighthearted font for the kids. Monogram soaps and finger towels add a touch of class in powder rooms.

- **THE KITCHEN**. Coasters, cutting boards, and coffee mugs all wear the family moniker well. We have an ergonomic single-letter *C* monogram floor mat by our kitchen sink, which offers function and form, classing up the kitchen while taking some of the backache out of doing dishes.

- **THE BEDROOM**. Here's the perfect place for a couple to display a duogram. I have MCD stitched on our pillowcases and main accent pillow. Whitman has seen couples put their individual monograms, or just their first initials, on their respective pillow shams, and their duogram on the duvet cover. For the grandkids now coming along, we had individual pillow shams made with their names on them. Whoever is coming to stay has his or her name on the bed when they arrive. It's one more way to let all the kids know they belong here.

- **THE LIVING ROOM**. Some households design a monogram so it serves as a family logo or crest, and use the stylized lettering the same way in all applications, which works well on throw pillows for the living and family rooms, or for serving trays on the coffee table.

- **DON'T OVERDO IT**. You get the idea, but curb your enthusiasm. "One or two monogrammed items per room is enough," Whitman recommends. "Too much overwhelms."

16

The Kids Are All Right

In the United States today, the intact, biologically bonded family composed of a mother, father, and children is no longer the rule. The recoupled family *is*, according to Dr. Jeannette Lofas, president and founder of the Stepfamily Foundation, and author or coauthor of five books on step-families, including *Living in Step* (1976, with Ruth Roosevelt), and *How to Be a Step Parent* (1989).

"Today, 60 percent of families live in some form of divorced or stepfamily relationship," she said, where one or both partners have children from a prior marriage. These children may live with their parent full-time, part-time, or just visit. In America, 1,300 new stepfamilies form every day.

Thus, when couples merge lives and furniture, they are also very often blending kids. While I will leave navigating those dynamic waters to the psychology types, this much I know: Regardless of whether the children live with you full-time or part-time, whether they're off to college or have their own place, whether they visit daily or only on holidays, every child needs to feel—and see—that they have a place in the home.

WHERE DO I FIT IN?

That is the central question kids need answered when they see their families transformed. They want to know if they have a place in the new family, and where that is. The parent's job is not only to *say* but to *show* these kids that the answer is unequivocally *yes*. That answer will come through in how you set up the home.

Here are eight ways to make sure the kids feel at home:

I. PROVIDE EQUAL REPRESENTATION.

You may not notice that you have all your daughter's soccer trophies and memorabilia on display but precious little reflecting your partner's daughter's debate championships, but the kids will notice. Even if one child acts as if he or she doesn't care—don't believe it. You do not have to create a shrine to your kids, but you do have to showcase or represent each child evenly.

2. DISPLAY PHOTOS WITH INTENTION.

Although you may have one child who is camera shy and another who loves the limelight, be sure the photos on display show all offspring equally. The family photo wall or table is very symbolic, and is an opportunity to show the blended family coming together. The kids will be looking, believe me, at how they fit in, and who's most prominent. If all photos can share similar frames, that also makes a statement.

A man I know, a father of two, got remarried to a woman who has three kids. All the kids were grown and out of the house. The man moved into the woman's fully furnished house, and took almost none of his own furnishings. Instead, he put his belongings, including his photos, in storage. When his kids visit his new home, they see only large portraits of the new wife's children, and no pictures of them. They feel hurt every time.

Before Kristin Wann Anderson of Utah got remarried, she had two oil portraits of her children hanging in her dining room. She took the paintings down after the marriage in 2014 because her husband didn't have anything comparable of his kids. That is the right lens. (You'll learn more about Kristin's blended home in chapter 20.)

In our home, the photo table in the family room and an adjacent shelf have photos that feature all five kids, and now four grandkids. All are in silver frames so they "go together." In the center of the table is our wedding picture, where all our kids flank DC and me. To me, that is the heart of our home, our central statement: We are blended.

3. CREATE A SPACE FOR THEM.

Until kids grow up and are completely out of the home and well on their way, every child should have a place in the house that is just theirs. This doesn't have to be a room but can be a shelf, a chest, a desk, a drawer or two, according to design psychologist Dr. Toby Israel. The space needs to be respected. Don't violate it by putting other things there when they're not around. This provides their tether to the house, and is psychologically important.

"We've found that the amount of stuff or the size of the space one controls doesn't matter so much as the feeling that you have control over your things," says Dr. Michelle Janning, the sociology professor from Whitman College. "If you start to get invaded, that is an important sign of a problematic power dynamic."

4. INCLUDE THEM IN THE HOUSEWORK.

The key to making kids feel like part of the household is to not treat them like guests, says Jeannette Lofas, a stepchild and stepmother herself. Everyone has a job. One person makes the salad. Another empties the dishwasher. Someone else sets the table. Everyone cooks. Being part of a family means taking part in the running of the household, and not sitting on the sidelines.

5. CREATE RITUAL EVENTS.

Traditions are part of what defines a family. Creating new or continuing old family traditions with new family members goes a long way toward knitting blended families together. One small way we work to build a network among our kids, who live in four states, is by sending a group text on every member's birthday. That way, everyone can send a warm wish, which serves as a secondary reminder of the extended blended family we all belong to.

6. SHOW RESPECT.

You can't make blended family members love one another, but you can teach them to respect each other. Dr. Marilyn Coleman, professor of human development and family science at the University of Missouri, says a common problem she runs across is when men complain about the lack of respect their new wives have for their belongings and for their children's things.

One man told Coleman that his wife wanted to throw out all of his Christmas decorations, which were his and his child's connection to the holiday. Another complained that his wife put all of his beloved Western-style furniture in his daughter's room and would allow none of it in the rest of the house.

"The underlying message, aside from insinuating that he had no taste," said Coleman, "was the disrespect for his daughter, who had no say in the matter." These are power struggles that don't bode well for the new family, she added. "Compromise was not a part of their marital strategy. I think most couples don't think about these 'minor' things as the power struggles that they are."

Couples who do run into these sorts of struggles as they begin a merger probably need to settle them through therapy, she said. "A good therapist will help them realize that the Christmas decorations or the furniture are not the real issues."

Most important, someone needs to make sure the child is heard. For younger kids, the parent should listen and advocate. The parent needs to mediate between the child and the stepparent, without letting the kid become a divisive tyrant, but also without allowing the new partner to disregard the child's feelings. Adolescents are typically quite good at advocating for themselves and, sadly, the parent often backs them up without talking to the stepparent. "That is another reason for therapy," says Coleman. "It may take an objective outsider to help the couple (and the child) learn to deal with the situation."

7. REASSURE THEM.

When adults remarry and merge households, they sometimes get so caught up in their own life transitions that they forget the ripple effect on their families. Take time to both show and tell the kids: There will always be a home for you here.

8. CELEBRATE THE LESSONS.

"Family is where we learn, and that is especially true in blended families," says Lofas. "Blended families teach us there are thirty ways of looking at the world. They teach important life lessons, like how to adapt and assimilate, and also that everyone can bring you something. They offer much to celebrate."

PART FOUR

How They Did It

Six blended households—some couples, some families—share their tales from the homefront and discuss what did and didn't work.

17

Sara and Austin: Letting Go and Holding On

When couples start getting cozy, the question soon becomes, "Your place or mine?" As they get cozier, the question then becomes, "Your stuff or mine?" As any established adult who has merged with another has found, hearts merge more easily than households.

Sara Nation, of Douglas County, Colorado, would be among the first to agree.

When I first talked to Sara in July 2017, the then fifty-nine-year-old program manager for a large health system had just moved in with her committed partner, Austin Tilghman, a sixty-five-year-old bank consultant. The couple, both divorced, had met at a charity event six years earlier. She owned a 3,800-square-foot (353 sq m) home, where she had lived for fifteen years and raised her three children. His house was more than twice that size, and had been home to his ex-wife and their two children, as well. That's a lot of sofas and chairs.

Because they wanted a fresh start in a place neither had lived in, they moved into a rental house until they could decide to either buy a house or build one.

Austin sold his house, which had been decorated with Tuscan villa–style furnishings to suit the architecture. Sara rented her house out to her son, and brought her contemporary-style furnishings with her. Now she and Austin were shoehorning their edited belongings from more than 12,000 square feet (1,115 sq m) of combined houses into a 4,500-square-foot (418 sq m) cottage-style rental home. You do the math.

Beyond the obvious problem of having enough furniture to outfit a place three times that size, her contemporary furniture clashed with his Tuscan-villa pieces, and neither suited the cottage-style rental.

"I thought we had gotten rid of a lot and downsized enough, but we're not even close," she told me two weeks after they'd moved in. "I'm still struggling with where to put stuff."

Adding to the general chaos, Sara's thirty-two-year-old daughter, who was going through a job change, moved in. "So, we have my stuff, his stuff, and her stuff," Sara said. "I'm dizzy thinking about it. Nothing matches. The whole place is a mishmash of furniture and art that doesn't go and doesn't fit the cottage-style house. You don't walk in and say, 'Ahh, this is home, and I'm happy to be here.'"

The challenge became how they could live there for ten months to a year until they found the house they wanted to be in for twenty years or more. "Until I know what that looks like, it doesn't make sense to buy furniture, or let any go," said Sara. "However, between now and then, I need some beauty and comfort. I need to come home to a house I like again. I'm feeling a lot of anxiety just looking at the different styles of furniture, a mash-up of three lives in transition, and I need to make it work."

The tension had taken a toll on her disposition, she confessed. "I have not been a nice person," she said. "I yelled at Austin for the first time in my life two days ago."

What triggered the outburst was that he'd crossed a line. He had moved his office stuff into the space they'd declared would be her home office. That was already pushing it. Then he told a friend of his, who was staying with them, that he could use Sara's office to make phone calls.

"I felt very violated. I work from home eight to ten hours a day. I felt that he had no respect for my area," she said. "He moved his stuff out. He heard me. I felt really bad."

But they learned a lesson: Blending and downsizing involves making compromises and setting boundaries. "One boundary is that we both need our own space. Some places are sacrosanct, and you need to carve those out."

As for the furniture surplus, Sara has the right attitude. "It's not that we have trouble letting go of old belongings," she said. (Pause right there for a round of applause.) "We're happy to leave the past behind and are very excited about the next chapter. We just don't know what that looks like, so we don't know what to keep."

"What do you want for sure?" I asked.

"We have one piece of art that we both love, which we bought together. That's it," she said.

"Sounds like a good start to me," I said.

She thought a bit more, then added, "And I have an antique chair that was my grandfather's, which I want no matter what. The chair is carved wood and is covered in old sturdy fabric, just like him. And Austin really likes his large brown leather ottoman."

I could hear the wheels turning, and was curious to see how it would all shake out.

Almost two years later . . .

In April 2019, I called Sara back. The merger was going slower than expected. They were still in the rental but were moving out in a month into a house they had bought and had been renovating. The daughter had moved out and was now renting Sara's old house, since the son had moved out. Some furniture went with her.

"I never imagined we'd be in the rental two years," Sara said. But it had been time well spent. Sara and Austin had worked together to answer some critical questions, including where they wanted to live and what their combined style would look like. They'd also continued to downsize, letting pieces go to family members and friends as they looked for their next forever home.

"Looking ahead twenty years, we weren't sure if we wanted to live downtown near culture, the arts, and good restaurants, or outside the city, with open space, beautiful scenery, and nature around us." They chose the latter, in a gated community where their current rental was.

With that decided, Sara realized that if she was going to make this community home, she needed to put down some roots and invest herself in the place. In 2018, at age sixty, she'd retired to do just that.

"Austin had been trying to get me to retire for a long time, but I had worked for almost forty years so that was hard. However, I knew I couldn't make a new circle of friends and get acclimated into our community working the way I had been," said Sara.

With the location resolved, and a dedicated commitment to place, they began house hunting. They initially looked at patio homes. The idea of less house and less maintenance appealed. Ultimately, though, they decided they wanted more room to entertain family and friends, and more land around them.

After a year, Sara and Austin found a 5,000 square-foot (465 sq m) house, about the same size as their rental, on the tenth hole of the community's golf course. Initially, they planned to move right in after they put in new wood floors and replaced the windows, but the minor remodel turned into a total gut. "It snowballed into new everything. We have changed the look and feel of the house entirely," said Sara. The new home is a style she describes as "modern mountain and 100 percent us." It will have an office for Austin and an art studio for Sara, who, once the house project is over, wants to paint more now that she's retired.

The disagreements have almost disappeared, Sara said of the renovation project. "At this stage of our lives, we're more flexible. He's put his foot down on certain choices, and so have I, but it hasn't been difficult to agree on how the house will look and feel."

The process forced them to define their combined style and then to take a second hard look at their combined furnishings and decide which pieces they could see moving forward.

"We now know we'll move in with very little of our former furniture, and we're okay with that," she said. They will take their bed, which they bought jointly after moving in together, and a guest bedroom set, which was Sara's, but most items are not moving with them, including the art they bought together and, yes, her grandfather's chair.

The art, which pictured a vineyard, went well with the Tuscan furniture, Sara said, but didn't go with the modern mountain vibe. The traditional brown leather ottoman also was let go.

And the chair?

"I look at that chair now," said Sara. "It's fifty-plus years old. I still remember sitting on my grandfather's lap in that chair. And that memory will stay with me. But the chair looks tired. I could reupholster it, but that would change it a lot." She eventually saw that the chair really wouldn't fit. After asking herself whether it was worth working around, worth holding on to when it wouldn't go with the rest of the house, she let it go.

The irony that they had started with three times the furniture they "needed" and they were now moving forward with almost none was not lost on her. But she thinks she knows why she holds on to things a little less tightly than most people.

HARD-WON LESSON

Sara's ability of letting go to move forward is admirable, and also hard-won. She'd lost everything before. Twice.

The first time, she was in her twenties. While between moves, she'd temporarily stored all her belongings in a basement that flooded. Everything was ruined. Twenty years later, while living in a house she owned, she lit a candle in a room with an open window, stepped away, and returned to find the room in flames. She and her pets got out. But as she sat across the street waiting for the fire department, she watched her entire house burn down, taking everything with it.

"Those experiences got me to where I am today," she said. "So much of our stuff simply doesn't matter. I have what I really need."

She is grateful for where she is, if a little impatient. "We are over the moon about our future. We have felt like we were in limbo for so long. We are finally really beginning our lives together. It has all been worth the wait."

Sara's Advice

- **BE WILLING TO COMPROMISE.** It's all for the bigger picture, the shared vision. But if you're truly committed to a place or a piece of furniture, work it in.
- **REMEMBER WHY YOU'RE HERE.** "After waiting all these years to find the person I wanted to spend the rest of my

life with, everything else was easy," she said. "We make decisions together with the goal of making each other happy."

THE "FOR NOW" TRAP

"Don't fall into the trap of 'for now,'" said professional organizer Ben Soreff, of House to Home Organizing in Norwalk, Connecticut, when I shared Sara Nation's story with him. "Families in flux too often make the mistake of labeling a living situation as temporary. Life is a constant state of flux. You assume the child will get a job, or the parent will move to assisted living, or your new house will be built soon. Then a year goes by, and no one feels integrated."

Rather than put up with disarray, "lean into the situation and forget the temporariness," said Soreff. "If you don't, no one feels settled." Clutter and resentment build when people don't have enough space. Everything is temporary. Make *now* nice.

Elaine and Mike: Uptown Girl Meets Downtown Guy

"Finding the right house might be more of a challenge than finding the right man!" I was on the phone with my friend, interior designer Elaine Griffin. She was cracking me up, as usual. We were commiserating about how hard it is to make two homes one, never mind making two hearts one; that's the easy part.

We are so there.

In August 2017, Elaine was happily engaged and unhappily house hunting. "Though I've found the man of my dreams, finding the house of our dreams is proving . . . uhh . . . interesting," she said. "It really is easier to merge souls than households."

Knowing laughter all around.

"Single people are used to being the commanders of their space," she said. "They're in charge of what happens where. It's one thing to invite someone to visit your kingdom, but quite another when one person moves in, or you get a place together. Then . . . welcome to mayhem."

She's just confirmed my theory that cohabitating tests the best relationships. "The older you get, the harder it gets," she added. But they're determined.

Elaine and Mike, a car dealership owner, started dating in November 2015. Almost two years later, the couple, who are both in their fifties, decided to find a house and get married—in that order.

Elaine's large home in coastal Georgia was also her childhood home. "Living there would feel creepy to him," said Elaine. Mike, a divorced father of four, lives in a condo with two bedrooms plus a loft nearby but closer to town. "There's no room for me there."

So they're looking. She wants big. He wants practical.

"The house Mike would ultimately want would be too small for me," she said. What's more, she likes uptown. He's more downtown. Yet they are both bent on finding a place they love. "It has to happen!" she says. "We can't set a wedding date until we've found the house."

"How does your furniture get along?" I dared ask.

"Oh, my Lord!" she cried, then parodied their conversation: "*Your soul, darling, is easy to love. Your sofa on the other hand . . .*"

More hysterical laughter.

She has a Louis XVI settee. He has an enormous leather sectional with cup holders (!).

"Opposites attract," I said. "What about art?"

Another big burst of laughter. Elaine then shared an example. She has a collection of eighteenth-century picture frames—just frames, with no art in them. "They're beautiful and cultural. I like to hang them as a grouping." Mike cannot figure out why on earth she would hang empty frames. "He'll say, 'Can't you put something in there?' and I'll say, 'No!'"

The only way to get what you want is to stay single, she added. "Once you say I do, or make a commitment, it's compromise city."

Nineteen Months Later . . .

In spring 2019, I called Elaine to hear how it had worked out. They had found a place, a beautiful 3,500-square-foot (325 sq m), four-bedroom home. In May 2018, they moved in. The house was close to town, which Mike appreciated, and big enough to absorb them and Mike's youngest son, a teenager who still lived with him part-time. Both held on to their prior homes.

"We leased the house with the option to buy if all went well," said Elaine, who had every reason to believe it would. By now, they had been together three-and-a-half years.

By August, Mike had moved out.

"The bottom fell out," she said. "We had a meltdown. It just didn't work. We had different parenting styles and different lifestyles."

Elaine, who divorced in 2012 after a brief marriage, has no children. For her, having a teenager in the home was a big adjustment. She and the son did not always see eye to eye. Plus the fact that Elaine likes a grander lifestyle and

LIVING APART TOGETHER

When couples have conversations about what life will look like in the same shared space and realize there's no way forward, or if they discover their relationship doesn't fit the mold, that is not a failure in any way, shape, or form, says Indianapolis sociologist and cohabitation expert Dr. Amanda Miller. "You can decide not to waste each other's time, or agree to get married and live apart."

Dr. Michelle Janning agrees, and adds, "In fact, the older we get, the less inclined we are to start something new, the more we think, 'I need to protect myself and my assets.'"

This is why the LAT trend—Living Apart Together—is on the rise, she said. More partners are keeping separate spaces because they want to keep their own homes and their own things. They don't want to pick up after anyone else, or fight the thermostat wars, or put up with the snoring.

"The bottom line is that people will do what they need to do for relationships," said Janning.

Mike likes a simpler life also became a wedge. Altogether, a schism formed that they could not close.

Mike moved back to the condo. Elaine stayed in the leased house until January 2019, when it sold. "There was a time we didn't speak to each other."

By the time I talked to her, she'd come full circle and was back living in her old childhood home with a new perspective. She and Mike were dating again, though a marriage was not in the making. "We learned we can't live together."

A failure, though, isn't a mistake. "Though living together didn't work for us, it wasn't a mistake," said Elaine. "We're still together, and we're better for it. We took a breather and we're stronger. When you're set in your ways, it's okay to surrender to the hard relationship truth that sometimes your lifestyles are just not suited for cohabitation, and that's okay."

Can she see it working out in the future? That would be a *no*. "If we ever did get a place together down the road, it would be for weekends only."

More laughter.

Here are her tips:

Elaine's Advice

- **LEASE BEFORE YOU BUY**. "I strongly encourage every mature couple to start by leasing. Give it six months to see if it really works. For us, it didn't."

- **KEEP EXIT RAMPS OPEN**. Not that you go into this with one foot out the door, but be realistic here. Give it a year. Mike had hung on to his condo. Elaine still had the family home on the coast. Have an exit plan.
- **HAVE A REFUGE**. The secret to making a blended home work is making sure each person has his or her own space. Each person has to have a refuge, where they can close the door and be alone.
- **KNOW YOURSELF**. The bar for what you will tolerate in someone when you're in your twenties is a lot lower than it is when you're older.
- **DON'T THROW THE BABY OUT WITH THE BATHWATER**. Just because living together didn't work out, doesn't mean the relationship is over. The dream of the white picket fence is not for everybody. Not being able to live together doesn't mean the other person isn't the one for you. Your forever partner might not be your forever roommate.

19

Sherry, Rachel, and Michael: All in the Family

One evening while Rachel and Michael Tidwell were visiting Rachel's mom, Sherry, who lived a few blocks away, one offhand remark changed their lives.

"We were sitting around my kitchen table," recalls Sherry Lopatic, of that fateful night in January 2016, "bemoaning all the recurring bills we both had to pay—lawn maintenance, cable, alarm systems—when I said jokingly, 'It's ridiculous. We should just live together.'"

To her and her daughter's surprise, Rachel's husband, Michael, was to first to say, "Absolutely!"

What man volunteers to live with his mother-in-law? A very special one.

"Actually," Michael told me later, "the same thought had been in the back of my mind. We already spent so much time together. It just made sense."

When Rachel got her husband alone, she applied a hand to his forehead and asked if he meant it. The idea quickly gained traction.

REDEFINING THE BLENDED HOME

Two months later, Rachel and Michael, both in their early thirties, moved, with their cat and three dogs, out of their three-bedroom, 1,400-square-foot (130 sq m) house into Sherry's three-bedroom, 1,500-square foot (139 sq m) one-story house in Midwest City, Oklahoma, with her cat and two dogs. This was supposed to be for just a few months while the couple sold their house, and they all looked for a new place.

What could possibly go wrong?

As the only child of a single mother, Rachel says she and her mom are "exceptionally close."

Michael said that when he married Rachel ten years ago, "I knew it would be a package deal." But no one ever assumed that would mean all being in the same house.

They weighed family dynamics and benefits. "If my son-in-law weren't so easygoing, I would have never considered this," said Sherry, who's in her late fifties, long divorced, and recently retired from a thirty-five-year government job as a security specialist.

"If children come along, mom will be here to help with them," said Rachel. "Plus, by combining our resources, we knew we could get a home now that otherwise we would not be able to afford for a long time."

As Sherry looked ahead, she knew she'd come to appreciate living on one level, and the security of not living alone. Looking even further ahead, she reasoned, "If we went in together and got a bigger house, they would have that now and also when I'm gone."

While the Tidwells would give up a little privacy, Sherry would make the biggest adjustment, downsizing to a mother-in-law suite, ultimately a space less than one-third the size of the house she had all to herself.

"I didn't do it overnight," she said. "I spent some weeks sitting in my packed garage, surrounded by all this stuff I'd hung on to. I had to start asking, do I really need all this? I knew mentally I should get rid of it, but my heart didn't want to. It was hard."

Sherry had slowly been downsizing her home even before the talk of moving, so she was mentally getting ready. Rachel and Michael, however, were still in acquisition mode.

The Tidwells' house sold quickly, and there was no turning back. The trio began looking for a house in the 2,500-square-foot (232 sq m), $250,000 price range. They wanted the mother-in-law suite, a large yard for the dogs, and a location just outside the city but not too far from their jobs. Rachel works in human resources for the school district, and Michael is a banking executive.

They looked. And they looked. Nothing checked all the boxes.

When the few months of living together became ten, they decided that the only way to get exactly what they wanted was to build it. They bought an acre of land in Oklahoma County and broke ground in March 2017. The following October, after eighteen months of living together in Sherry's house and storing their furniture in the garage, they moved into their new four-bedroom 3,000-square-foot (279 sq m) house, which also has an additional 400-square-foot (37 sq m) attic bonus room.

Though they ended up spending closer to $350,000 for more house, they all believed they came out ahead. But they wouldn't know for sure until after they had moved in and lived together for a while.

One Year Later . . .
Painted on a large mirror in the breakfast nook of their house is the word *Together*. It's a fitting motto for Sherry, Rachel, and Michael, who had lived in their merger project for about a year when I checked back with them.

"How's that working out?" I wanted to know.

"The upside is so great," Rachel said. "We have a much better place, and aren't spending as much."

But what I really wanted to know was how all the furniture got along.

"You would think that since we were going from two houses that totaled 2,900 square feet to one house with a little more space, there wouldn't be any problems," said Rachel, "but there were many."

Though their three personalities meshed nicely, and their blended pet family of five dogs and two cats got along, their combined furniture . . . not so much.

"Believe me, deciding whose furniture and decorations would go where—or just go—was a challenge," Sherry said. She furnished her 450-square-foot mother-in-law suite on the main floor with her things. Some of her other furnishings, they agreed, would go in the main area of the house.

Michael, who was gunning for son-in-law of the year, wisely left those discussions to the women. "I had no strong feelings about any of it," he said. Well, except for the dining room table—the contemporary bar-height dining room table was a favorite of Michael's. "We'd just bought it, and it was nonnegotiable," said Rachel.

Sherry argued that a high table would be harder when children came along. "Plus," she said, "it wasn't my style." She wanted to use her dining room table.

"That's when I pulled my card," said Rachel, "and said, 'Well, it won't be going in your area.'"

"I gave in a little more," said Sherry, "because I had my area where I could do what I wanted." However, both sides made sacrifices.

Sherry also wanted to keep her retro Formica diner-style kitchen table with red vinyl chairs. "I really, really liked that table and chairs. Although I knew it didn't fit the new decor, if it had been just me, I would have made it work."

Sherry held firm, however, to her open-shelved pine hutch. "It was one of my favorite things, and was coming no matter what," she said. Today, the hutch has a featured place in the family room.

Once they'd hashed out what would go where, they held a huge garage sale, where Sherry sold probably 60 to 70 percent of her stuff, including her well-used sectional, the retro kitchen table and chairs, her dresser, and her queen-size bed. She bought a double that fits better.

Looking back on their year of transition, Sherry sums it up like this: "All in all, it was a good move. We still have discussions, like, when holidays come around and we need to decide on that season's decorations, but no blood has been shed and we are living peacefully and happily—together."

Rachel and Sherry's Advice

"Merging households isn't for every family, but it works for us," said Rachel, who with her mom offers the following advice for anyone considering blending households:

- **CONSIDER THE TRADE-OFFS.** Because they were moving from six bedrooms to four, both women lost their home offices. Now Sherry has a desk and printer table in her mother-in-law suite; Rachel makes do with a desk in the kitchen. Sherry also mourns the loss of her walk-in closet. But they all like living in a nicer house with consolidated payments.

- **TAKE A TEST DRIVE.** Try living together temporarily before committing. Living together for eighteen months in a smaller house was a good stress test for this trio, who concluded that if they could make that work, they could definitely make the larger place work. "At first it felt strained," said Rachel. "We felt like it was her house and we couldn't make it our home. I worried that strain would come into the new house. But it didn't. In fact, the new house is big enough that often we don't see each other all evening."

- **BRACE FOR JUDGMENT.** What surprised Rachel most was the judgment from others. "People assume you are doing this because you're not doing well enough. They say, 'Oh, your mother lives with you?' and think, 'Did something go wrong?'" No, actually, something went right.

- **TALK ABOUT THE LONG TERM.** When considering blending households, talk about down-the-road matters, like if kids come along, aging in place, privacy, and boundaries. "We talked through everything, including who would pay what," said Rachel. "We left no room for fighting. Today, whenever there's a minor grievance, that is quickly swept away when we say, 'Look at what we have.'"

- **SYNC YOUR STYLE.** Sherry and Rachel share similar tastes in decor, which helped a lot. "If I had a chrome-and-glass modern daughter, we wouldn't have even tried," said Sherry.

- **HEAD ARGUMENTS OFF AT THE DOOR.** The women created a scaled floor plan and made cutouts of furniture pieces to scale to decide what would go where long before the movers came. So most arguments were waged and resolved beforehand.

- **VETO POWER.** Besides letting each party claim a few nonnegotiable items to keep, both sides also had a limited number of vetoes. Each person had a right to say, "That absolutely is not going in."

- **COMPROMISE.** "One of our main disagreements was over blinds," said Sherry, who wanted them on every window. Rachel was adamant about not having blinds. They settled: Sherry has them in her area, but there are none in the rest of the house.

- **SOMETIMES THE ANSWER IS "NEITHER."** Because neither party had furniture that fit the main living area, they sold their sofas and sectionals, and Rachel and Michael bought a new sofa, love seat, and oversized chair that fit right in.

- **KEEP YOUR PERSPECTIVE.** "Ask yourself," said Sherry, "how important, in the scheme of things, getting your way really is, and if it's worth having tension in the house because the other person's furnishings bother you." If you decide to blend, you need to bend.

THE ACCORDION HOUSEHOLD

Often the impetus behind blending—or not blending—a home is financial, says sociology professor Amanda Miller. "Many of the working-class couples we interviewed had experienced what we call an accordion household," she said. These are homes where boomerang kids come back, or a parent moves in. "These households expand and contract to meet social and emotional needs."

In accordion households, those at the core are the stable adults, flexing in and out. With mature couples, the challenges come when you have this quasi-step family, said Miller, and your new husband's twenty-six-year old daughter, whom you never parented.

To navigate these waters, according to Miller, couples need to have "some very intentional conversations ahead of time, not as the situations come up, and ideally prior to moving in." Before moving in, discuss very clearly whether any of you anticipate anyone else moving in, and if so who, why, and for how long. Discuss how you will set ground rules, including time limits, chores, and finances.

20

Rebecca and Dean, Kristin and Rich, Jason and John

As we've seen, merging into a new home with a new partner involves a lot of give and take. However, when one partner moves into the other's domain, the dance is even more delicate. Though, ideally, the couple would agree to clear out the home and start fresh, real life rarely complies.

Here are three stories of couples where one partner moved into the other's home, along with what they learned in the process.

REBECCA AND DEAN: ALL FOR THE DOG

After dating for eleven years, Rebecca Kuma and Dean Stills, both in their late forties, had discussed living together on many occasions. "We get along very well, and are financially independent," said Rebecca. But what really tipped the scales was Bambi, a two-year-old Chihuahua-terrier mix they rescued in 2017.

"She stole our hearts and brought us closer," said Rebecca. "We were going back and forth like we shared custody." Not anymore. In August 2018, she moved into Dean's 2,400-square-foot (223 sq m), four-bedroom, three-bath house in a suburb of Orlando, which he shared with his fifteen-year-old daughter.

Of the two of them, Dean (the upholsterer we met in chapter 12) had the larger home. Rebecca, a business consultant who has never been married and has no kids, lived in a two-bedroom townhome, which she owned and could rent out. So when the couple decided to live under one roof, the question of whose place was easy. The question of whose stuff was more challenging. "We went around," said Dean. "She fought tooth and nail for some things."

Ultimately, Dean's stuff won out. "We left my furniture because it fit the style of the home better. I'm in the business and I have an eye," said Dean, who describes his tastes as more modern, while Rebecca's is more traditional. "She had a lot of heavy iron and oak."

As a result, the main house has not changed a lot since she moved in. "We were lucky. I had everything, and she didn't fight me. It worked out pretty fluidly," said Dean.

Was there anything she really wanted?

"I wanted my bedroom set because it was nicer," said Rebecca, "but it is currently in storage along with my couches. Dean is even more attached to his stuff than I am, so I just go with it."

Dean did build a new bed for them and they bought a new mattress, for their shared master. "When two people come together, that's something they want fresh," he said.

Rebecca left some furniture in the townhome to the renter. She also donated a few pieces to the local women's center. "Letting go was difficult," said Rebecca. "As I get older, I am more attached to everything. It helped that Dean has nice stuff, but currently the only furniture in the house that's mine is my office furniture." She also displays some drawings her dad made. However, they are making home improvements jointly and talking about future changes, which is helping Rebecca feel represented in the house.

"I know how I would feel if we'd moved into her place," said Dean. "I would feel like this doesn't feel like my place. That gives me empathy. So every time she says she wants to change something in the house so she can feel more a part of it, it's fine. I say, 'Whatever makes you happy.'"

"Dean also welcomes my mom to visit at any time and makes her feel at home," Rebecca said.

Living with Dean's daughter has not been a big adjustment, because Rebecca has been in the girl's life since she was four. "It also helps that Dean is such a good dad," said Rebecca. "I do not have to be a parent, just a good role model and help when needed."

One day they hope to buy a place at the beach, and maybe they'll use her furniture then, Dean said. "Where you're living now isn't where you'll always live."

The fact that she still owns her rental is her "security blanket," said Dean, who has been divorced twelve years. "By the time you get to be our age, you see the strings behind the curtain. You know what can happen."

Rebecca's Advice

- **TALK ABOUT EVERYTHING FIRST.** Discuss kids, parents, dogs, and anyone else who might share the home. Also talk about furniture, house payments, bills, schedules, and cleaning.
- **FIND YOUR COMPROMISE.** If both parties agree that one person's furniture fits the home better, the other partner may need to cede. But the trade-off should be that the partner who gives way has significant say in future purchases and improvements.

■ ■ ■

KRISTIN AND RICH:
IS THERE ROOM FOR ME?

When Kristin Wann Anderson downsized from her 4,600-square-foot (427 sq m) house in 2009, eight years after her divorce and the year her youngest went off to college, she was setting herself up for the life she envisioned, a life on her own. "This was going to be my home forever," said Anderson, then in her late fifties.

Her new 2,800-square-foot (260 sq m) house in Salt Lake Valley put her closer to the University of Utah School of Medicine, where she headed the alumni association. But life had other plans. An old boyfriend she'd dated in college came back into her life. A future together seemed unlikely.

Rich lived in Los Angeles, where he'd practiced medicine for thirty years. Not only was Rich's medical practice in Los Angeles, but also, so were three children, his parents, and his siblings. Kristin was firmly ensconced in Utah, where she'd gone to high school, and had a big network of friends. This was also home to her two children.

After two years of shuttling between Utah and California, the couple knew they wanted to be together. The question became where.

Rich had already sold his large family home in Glendale, and was renting a place, but that didn't mean he was ready to move from a life built over three decades. However, he said, "Kristin dug in over not moving to Los Angeles, so it was up to me to transplant."

Kristin convinced Rich she could find him a job working as a physician in the Salt Lake area. And he started thinking. "It took four to five months of serious reflection and lots of long hikes for my brain fog to clear to get to the point of moving," Rich said.

Therapy helped, too. "The therapy we did ahead of time helped me understand that, though it was hard for me to leave everything behind, it was just as hard for her to let me into her space. She had gone through her own divorce and all the garbage and come out the other side. I was not part of the plan."

In the fall of 2013, he packed up his life in Los Angeles and moved into Kristin's house in Salt Lake City. The couple married in August the following year.

Rich brought some antiques from his previous home. "I didn't need a whole lot," he said, "but I did need a few things that connected me to my life and family." Today, his favorite chair, a large Persian rug, some lamps, and his rolltop desk are all in the house. But some of the larger antiques he's still partial to are in the garage.

"He's been good about merging, and pretty good about saying what he wants," said Kristin.

And while both say the house—with mostly Kristin's furniture—still looks more like hers than his, they are grateful, respectful, and appreciative of what both have sacrificed and gained in the process.

"We both had first marriages that didn't work out, so we came in with our eyes more open," Rich said. "I recognized that she had re-created her life, and that her home was her space. When she moved into the home, she bought new furniture fitting her exact tastes. I wanted to honor that."

Yet, he also feels accommodated. "We do have a fair blend. Every room has something of mine or something we got together. I never feel like I don't belong," he said, though he's not ready to relinquish the antiques in the garage.

The House in Hindsight

As they worked through the merger, they often joked that they wished Kristin had held on to her bigger five-bedroom house. With a blended family of five grown children, the current home can feel a bit snug.

At one point, Kristin's daughter moved back home, followed by Rich's son. "At Christmas we had nine adults in various bedrooms and air mattresses all around. The kitchen was in constant turmoil with us all cooking large meals for five nights in a row."

"Nothing like moving into what you think will be your final home until assisted living comes to call, and then have your life turned upside down (in a good way) with a remarriage, more furniture and stuff descending on your (now our) home, along with a sudden increase in family size," said Kristin.

She and Rich are seriously discussing their next move— whether to find a new house that's a better fit, remodel the home they have, or live with it as is.

"We'd like to age in place, which means all necessary rooms on one level. I always want space for the kids and eventually grandkids to visit, and we want space for all the entertaining we like to do. We are looking for quality, not quantity. We know what we want, but we are so far unresolved," said Kristin.

Meanwhile, Rich is waiting in case the next iteration of home lets him get a few more antiques out of the garage.

Rich's Advice

- **GET THERAPY.** Go to counseling together, so you can see the situation from another viewpoint.
- **TALK HONESTLY.** Discuss all potential trigger points— money, sex, kids, and who pays for what.

- **FACTOR IN FAMILIES.** Don't underestimate the importance of making sure each other's kids like one another.
- **REMEMBER WHERE YOU CAME FROM.** When you've gone through divorce, you realize stuff is just stuff. Keep what's important foremost.

■ ■ ■

JASON AND JOHN: MAD ABOUT YOU

Step into the North Carolina home of Jason Oliver Nixon and John Loecke—owners of Madcap Cottage, an interior design and home products company—and the word that springs to mind is "exuberant." Known globally for their signature style, which is colorful, zany, whimsical, and fun, the couple mix paisley, plaid, patterns, and prints with abandon and aplomb. Which prompts the question: Were they both always like this? In fact, no.

"We were the odd couple," said Jason, referring back to 2000 when they decided to move in together. The couple was living in Manhattan working for magazines. They chose Jason's place—a 400-square-foot (37 sq m) one-bedroom apartment—because he owned his place and John was renting.

"I was a neatnik minimalist," Jason recalls. "John was more . . . relaxed, traditional, and eclectic."

Jason's apartment reflected his modern aesthetic: white walls; spare furnishings in neutrals; and only a few items of clothing, all in black.

"I don't think I owned a piece of black clothing," said John, whose traditional furniture and extensive wardrobe were far more colorful and—gasp!—patterned.

The clothes were among the first challenges. "John had like fifty-seven pairs of shoes and forty-three sweaters, to my two," said Jason. "We had two tiny closets, which I had to redo and make three levels. Thank goodness for the high ceilings."

Though Jason's style was far different from his, John acknowledged, "His place looked like a million bucks. Of all the people I knew in my age group, Jason had the most pulled-together place."

Fortunately, both were up for a change. The question became how could they take what they had to the next level and forge a new style? They started with a big purge.

On moving day, both vividly remember John's stuff all out on the sidewalk. "What are we going to do with all this [stuff]?" Jason had asked, and then mentioned a storage facility a block away.

"That was our compromise," said John. "I wasn't going to give up my stuff, but it wasn't going to work in that space." He put most of his belongings in storage, which he regrets. "I made a storage payment of about $150 month for twelve years for stuff I should have gotten rid of." He never used any of it again.

However, one piece he did move in to the apartment was a traditional rolled-arm upholstered chair, which he had slipcovered in a high-sheen pink toile chintz. "It was not clean-lined or modern," John said. "It was the complete opposite of Jason's apartment."

The Beginning of the Evolution

But the chair grew on Jason, and eventually was the seed to their blended design and to Madcap Cottage.

"Though I loved prints and patterns," Jason said, "I didn't know how to do with them what John did." He looks back at that first apartment as a time "that set us on a path personally and professionally. I had all that love of pattern in me, but it took that merger to bring it out."

John also credits Jason for the creative leaps they have made. "He allowed me to pull more influences from the worlds of travel and fashion," John said, "and to appreciate modern design."

The evolution, however, didn't happen overnight. It took years.

"Jason would have run screaming and our relationship would have ended if I had tried to do to his apartment what we ended up doing to our later homes," John said, offering hope to any couple blending households and going through the design wars.

"I was open, and John took me on an adventure, a journey of having fun with interiors that weren't all neutral," Jason said.

Today, their house, which is about ten times larger than that first apartment, reflects them.

"It's not a look you can quite pinpoint," John said.

"It's sort of England meets Palm Springs by way of Morocco," Jason said.

"It's us," John said.

John's Advice

- **GET A NEUTRAL PLACE**. If you can, avoid moving into a partner's home that doesn't come with baggage or preset decor. It's a lot easier to merge that way.
- **AVOID STORAGE AT ALL COSTS**. It is a black hole. We could have gone to Europe ten times for the money we wasted on storage. Do a deep edit, have a yard sale, and donate. If it's a family heirloom, send it to auction.
- **DON'T TRY TO MAKE YOUR BLENDED STYLE HAPPEN ALL AT ONCE**. Approach the process as an evolution.

Jason's Advice

- **BE OPEN TO THE ADVENTURE**. When you are open to the unexpected, that's when a bit of magic happens.
- **ACCEPT ENDINGS**. "I don't like to get rid of good furniture, but you have to recognize when a piece, like my high-style, low-comfort sofa, has run its course."

PART FIVE

The Crazy Quilt Family

As DC and I fumble through a series of blended holidays, we give our new blended family the ultimate test, discover the shortcomings of the Happy Yellow House, and find new meaning in "home for the holidays."

21

Redefining "Home for the Holidays"

I never set out to be the poster mom for blended families. DC and I were both married before, for happily ever after. His wife died. My marriage hit the rocks. And here we were, middle-aged newlyweds with a blended family of five (his three plus my two) more or less grown children.

Actually, we're a double-blended family. When DC married his first wife, she had a five-year-old son, so DC's eldest, Adam, is a stepson. So we are a mixed, colorful, bumpy, spread-out, crazy quilt of a family, which has enriched every member in countless and unimagined ways.

Since we married in 2016, life has been a series of new beginnings: new home, new marriage, new friends, new traditions. Wait. New traditions? Isn't that an oxymoron? *Tradition* by definition means old, as in you've done something the same way for yeeeeaaaarrrs.

How are we going to do that? As the female lead in this new ensemble, I believed the job of creating the holiday magic fell to me. We'd had a couple of bumpy trial runs getting the family together while we were courting, but as we celebrated our first married holidays together, I started looking around for the blended-family playbook and, finding none, I had to write it as we went.

When we got married, our kids ranged in age from twenty-one to thirty-six, and lived all over, scattered like dandelion seeds across four states. Getting them together was like expecting goldfish to line up when you blew a whistle.

Though they were all on board with the new deal, I could sense spines stiffening and heels rooting deeper, as we discussed just how and where and with whom everyone would spend the major holidays. (I believe one child suggested I spend them with my kids and DC spend them with his. To be fair, I could see how that made perfect sense.)

My ex-husband had also remarried, creating another set of stepsiblings. DC's two sons, Adam and Brett, were married, so had their wives' families to consider.

In other words, we were all writing new playbooks.

For our first married Thanksgiving, I had naturally presumed everyone would come to our house. However, a few inquiries soon revealed that the married offspring were planning to spend the holiday with their in-laws. Alyssa and Paige, who lived in Arizona and Texas, respectively, both had boyfriends, and didn't want to travel on a Thanksgiving weekend; they wanted to cook dinner in their own apartments. (Both invited us.) Marissa wanted to go to my brother's in California, because her college was nearest to him.

"I feel abandoned," I told DC.

"Be grateful we have independent kids who landed on their feet and have solid extended families."

"How could they not need me?" I cried. "Was it my mashed cauliflower that I tried to disguise as potatoes?" True, I did serve this for the Christmas dinner during our blended family's first combined holiday, which was probably a mistake. Meanwhile, my Norman Rockwell picture of everyone huddled around the turkey was turning to mincemeat pie.

Before I made a mama-sized mess out of this, I decided to call a pro. Dr. Donald Gordon is an expert in parent-child relationships, and founder of the Center for Divorce Education, in Ashland, Oregon.

"Humans crave predictability," said Gordon, when I asked him why traditions were so important to me. "Simple routines like getting up and making coffee are comforting, while a change in patterns is stressful. This repetition of pattern gets amplified on holidays, when expectations are high, and the potential for disappointment therefore great."

"I'm crestfallen and the season's first holiday isn't even here yet," I said.

"Holidays for blended families can be tricky, because they bring back memories of previous holidays that can never be again. People who have lost a loved one really feel it," he said. Returning "home" can actually magnify the feelings of loss.

Take a moment, please, and pause to feel this. It's okay.

"But how do you create old traditions in a new marriage, when everyone wants to go their own way?" I asked.

"It takes time."

THE BLENDED HOLIDAYS

Blended—I like to call them *remodeled*—families make up most families today, said Dr. Gordon. Though no two blended situations are the same, for those working to find a new holiday normal, here's some of his advice:

- **CONTINUE THE TRADITIONS YOU CAN.** Wherever you celebrate (and do consider going to an adult child's home), engage in at least one activity that you've always done on that holiday, said Gordon. Maybe you've always had Chinese takeout the night before Thanksgiving, or perhaps you all shoot pool, play board games, or take a long walk after dinner. Do those activities again. Then look for unique ways to build your own traditions in your new blended family.

- **MAKE THE MENU MEANINGFUL.** Food is the center of many traditions. Don't mess with expectations. Ask members across the aisle whether they have a traditional dish they'd like to have and make it, or have them make it. Meanwhile, introduce them to yours.

- **TUNE IN.** "Blended families cause swells of emotions, good and bad, for everyone involved," Gordon said. Kids often feel worried and anxious because they are trying to find their place in the new mix. "When you notice your kids are suddenly quiet, or moody, that's your cue to say, 'You look a little concerned.' Then listen. You want kids to know their feelings are legitimate and that it's good to talk them out," he said. "You can't always fix what's bothering them, but you can show you care and understand."

- **EMBRACE THE PRESENT.** Recognize and accept those feelings of missing what is no longer, but don't wallow. Swiftly shift your attention to the present and to what you're grateful for at the moment: the meal you're enjoying, the home you're in, the people you're with, the nature walk you take. Avoid ruminating over what's past. Traditions, like families, evolve in wondrous and unpredictable ways.

- **ENCOURAGE CONNECTION.** In a divorce situation, kids commonly miss the parent they're not with. Help your child connect with that parent or other absent family members through a phone call or FaceTime.

- **DON'T EXPECT A FAST WARMUP.** If kids don't warm up to the new spouse or stepsiblings right away, that's normal, said Gordon. "These relationships take a lot of years; bonding will happen in time. Don't push it."

- **LOWER YOUR BAR.** Happiness is the distance between our expectations and reality. If you heap a lot of expectations on the holiday, and it falls short, you will be unhappy. Maybe just say, *if I get to be with loved ones, that's enough.* "Look for what you're grateful for instead of focusing on not getting everything you want."

Passing the Torch

True, time marches on. I get that. But sometimes it lurches forward in giant whiplashing leaps, as it did on the first Christmas after we were married, which made me feel as if I'd aged a decade in one day.

That year, my two daughters felt they should see their dad in Colorado for the holiday. Meanwhile, DC's youngest son and his wife, who live nearest us in central Florida, were going to her parents' house.

DC's daughter, Alyssa, stepson Adam and his wife, Amber, and their two young children, Mason and Ariel, who all live in Arizona, wanted us to head their way for Christmas, which made more sense—logistically, at least—than having them all fly our way.

Insert heavy sobs here.

"What's wrong?" DC asked, when he saw my sad face, like a balloon with the air let out.

"I'm not ready to give up having Christmas at my house," I said.

"It's their turn," he said, squeezing my hand.

That was blow number one. For the first time since I had my children, they were not going to spend Christmas around my tree.

The second blow came with the realization that upon marrying DC, I instantly became a grandma.

"Am not," I'd told DC. "I am too young."

"Sorry," he said, "and no, you're not."

Ouch.

However, the little darlings call me Glamma, which, I admit, softens the blow.

When we arrived at the kids' house in Arizona, the grandkids, ages six and three, stormed the door. "G' Pa!" they shouted to DC, which he thinks makes him sound cool, like a rapper. "Glamma!" they'd squealed, which always melts me.

And there I was, spending Christmas Eve by someone else's tree—while the grandkids ran around restless with excitement and put out cookies for Santa and carrots for the reindeer—thinking how not so long ago, my girls were doing the same. I was trying not to feel too nostalgic, which I could not help, as I remembered holidays with my own mom, who'd died six months earlier but, thankfully, five months after seeing me remarry a wonderful man. She'd always made Scotch shortbread this time of year, so I baked a batch in my new daughter-in-law's kitchen, and taught her the family tradition. I felt myself stepping, I hoped gracefully, into a new role, which had taken me more than anyone by surprise, while my daughter-in-law asked for decorating advice, which I was honored and delighted to give. Suddenly, it struck me: I'd passed the torch. Ready or not.

After the season was over, and I'd had a chance to absorb these new blows, I'd learned a lesson every middle-aged, newly remarried stepmom and stepdad needs to know: Life moves. You can either go lightly, with the grace of a ballerina, or stubbornly, ungainly as a goat—but go you will.

As I fished around for more perspective, I began to appreciate how home life unfolds in chapters. From children, to newlyweds or partners, to parents or stepparents or aunts or uncles, maybe even to grandparents, we evolve. And then, in the wink of an eye, with the twist of a head, with a finger alongside the nose and a nod, time flies away like the down of a thistle, leaving you beside the next generation's tree, alongside close family, some of whom you may have just met.

Holidays in Step

When celebrating holidays for your expanding blended family, keep these thoughts in mind:

- **BE REALISTIC**. Newly married mature couples, kids of divorced parents, stepparents, and new step-grandparents, listen up: You cannot be in two places at once. Neither can your loved ones. So stop trying. Though you will likely feel pulled to please more than one household, keep guilt and stress to a minimum by accepting the reality that you cannot be everywhere and please everyone. When the holiday comes, celebrate the family members you are with, rather than mourn the ones who are absent.

- **BRIDGE WITH TRADITION**. Be intentional about making holiday decorations, recipes, and traditions from both sides of the aisle part of your celebration. Send everyone who doesn't live in the house the same holiday home accessory, maybe a festive table runner or an ornament, so they can share a connection with other family members, even if celebrating apart. Let everyone see both sides coming together with beauty, warmth, and acceptance.

- **FOCUS MORE ON THE PRESENT, LESS ON THE PAST**. The best way to weather the changes that come with the creation of a blended family is to adapt. Of course, you will reflect on past holidays, recall loved ones who are no longer around, and feel a twinge or two of melancholy.

When you find yourself dwelling on what is no longer, reframe that sadness with the positive thought of how fortunate you are to have those fond memories. Then focus on creating warm memories for those with you now. What happens now forms the memories of tomorrow.

- **PASS THE BATON**. Once children come on the scene, the torch inevitably gets passed from one generation to the next. For older parents, letting go can be tough, but put the younger ones first. You are now building their traditions. Go to them.

The holidays and New Year's force reflection on the passage of time and how families and our roles in them change, whether we're ready or not. For me, they also clarified what I deeply wanted and still didn't have.

22

From Downsized to Right-sized, Goodbye Happy Yellow House

I'm not sure when the wanderlust began. Maybe when we got a new puppy and became a two-dog family, or maybe when we finally sold my Colorado house, removing a burden and freeing some capital. Maybe the urge struck when we learned a fourth grandchild was on the way, or perhaps the blame lay in my compulsion to make a nest for my far-flung family to return to. My fantasy went something like this: *Maybe if we had a different house, everyone would visit more often, and I could better mend the inevitable fractures that occur when families of origin come apart.*

All I know is that one day, two years after DC and I moved into the Happy Yellow House, the house bug bit.

I did my best to quash the thought of moving. I, of all people, knew what lay ahead—the humbling hunt, the buy, the sell, the highs, the lows, the packing, the unpacking, the acid reflux, the insomnia, the thousand and one decor decisions, the broken budget, the broken fingernails, the sweating, the swearing, the renegotiating of all we'd negotiated.

Who in their right mind would want to go through that all over again? I think we both know the answer.

I secretly hoped DC would bring me to my senses, but he just made matters worse.

I probably started it by throwing out some test bait, like, "I wish we had one of those big kitchens with a counter and barstools that all the kids could sit around and shoot the bull while good smells come from the oven."

Rather than tell me to leave well enough alone, DC added, "I'd really like a yard for the dogs."

"I love our house, but a fireplace would be nice," I later added, piling onto our growing wish list of minor gripes, which grew to include, because, hey, no harm in just dreaming: A bigger dining room, a dedicated office for me, more room for our blended family to come and stay, more space to entertain—but all in the same great neighborhood. Oh, and in our price range.

Impossible, we thought, which was a relief.

Next, we tried doing what any homeowner on the rocks would do. We tried to work it out. We looked at our wish list to see whether we could add any of the upgrades to our Happy Yellow House. A room over the garage, perhaps? No matter, the result still fell short.

And so, the dream of a bigger place, with a larger kitchen, a yard, a fireplace, and a second office took hold. Soon we were "cheating" on our house, a house that we loved, that had been there for us, and that we were still so very fond of, but that, alas, left us wanting.

At first, we just looked, mostly online, and lusted. Wendy, our broker, sent us email alerts whenever a house in our price range came on the market or dropped in price.

I'd click through the listings, looking for flaws—master up, no fireplace, dated kitchen, funky layout, crummy street—so I could continue to say, "I still like our house better."

Then we started doing drive-bys. "I drove by that house on Pine today," DC would say almost sheepishly.

"So did I," I'd confess.

Next, we began sneaking out meeting other houses to see if we might have a future. I'd return to the Happy Yellow House feeling guilty and ungrateful, and do something nice for it, like polish the appliances or water the flowers, to make up.

One weekend when I was out of town, a stately Southern colonial right around the corner that we'd been eyeing— also a warm sunny yellow (was that a sign?)—dropped its price. DC went to see the property without me, which was safest. Afterword, he reported, in a tone of sober delight, "This house checks all our boxes."

A few days later, I saw it myself, and had one response: "Uh-oh."

A POINT OF CLARIFICATION

"You're moving from the Happy Yellow House?!" The questioning emails streamed in daily from readers of my column, editors, and friends when I broke the news. People I barely knew stopped me at church to ask, "Why?"

It was a legitimate question. I love that house. You love that house. It rescued me. How could we move? I owe you an explanation.

To refresh your memory, since we've come a long way since the beginning of this journey, over the prior six years and up to this point, I had called eight houses home. To recap: In 2011, I left house No. 1, the large home in Colorado, and moved to Florida for a new job and a new start. There, I landed a stint as a live-in home stager. Over the next four years, I would move into a series—six in all—of high-end houses that needed help selling, and stage them with my furniture. A few days after I'd moved into house No. 4, I had my first date with DC, who stabilized me like the anchor on the *Queen Mary*. We fell in love. By house No. 7, we were engaged. In June 2015, we bought house No. 8, the Happy Yellow House, where DC proposed in the kitchen the day we closed, and where we started our happily-ever-after life together. I had finally settled down, and the moving madness had ended.

Or so I thought.

Two short years later, we were looking to move. What happened? The short answer is: We undershot it.

Now, I know what you're thinking: "Isn't she the one who wrote *Downsizing the Family Home*? And now she's buying more house?" That is also a valid question, so let me clarify:

- **I AM NOT ALL ABOUT LIVING SMALLER.** I am about living better. I don't advocate for downsizing. I advocate for right-sizing, for having exactly as much house as you need, and no more. I want fit.

- **DOWNSIZING STUFF AND DOWNSIZING SPACE ARE NOT THE SAME.** Downsizing means living lighter, not necessarily smaller. It's about constantly pruning and weeding your belongings, as if tending a garden to make room for new growth. Life is not supposed to be a snowball of stuff that keeps growing as it rolls along.

- **LOCATION IS IMPORTANT, BUT FIT IS MORE IMPORTANT.** Our houses dictate how we live. As households expand or contract through marriage or divorce, through kids or parents coming or going, what you need in a home changes. Don't force your life to fit your home. Instead, if you can swing it, find a home that fits your life.

When DC and I bought the Happy Yellow House, it was perfect in so many ways, including being the ideal size for two empty nesters. I still remember the feeling, like an electric tree lighting up inside me, when I first walked in. The house's charming Mediterranean façade and romantic fountain in the back courtyard made me weak in the knees.

I was over the big house, which had weighed me down in Colorado. Our kids had all moved out, and we liked the idea of a smaller home. What we didn't anticipate was that although kids leave, they go and find mates and then multiply. Five becomes ten becomes fifteen. Four of our five had significant others, and the two married ones had created three more family members; another was arriving soon.

This was only going to go one way. If we wanted a place for extended family to gather—which we dearly did—we needed more room.

We also made some discoveries about each other after living together. Much as DC and I love our together time, we have separate interests that need space and walls and doors. I need a room to write, preferably not the same one he's using to watch the Steelers game. He needs room to play his electric guitar at 120 dB, if he feels like it. And he does.

So that is how we slowly, cautiously started looking at houses that had a little more elbow room, a little more yard, in the same wonderful neighborhood, in our price range. And that is how, one afternoon in late July 2017, DC came home with eyes like candle flames after he'd been to see a house, just nineteen houses away from where we lived.

The Happier Yellow House was larger by 800 square feet (74 sq m), 3,400 square feet (316 sq m) in all. It offered more bedrooms and more baths, a bigger kitchen, an office for me, a man cave for DC, and a yard for Peapod and Pippin, the new puppy. Because it needed a makeover—updated flooring, wall color, window coverings, light fixtures—all areas I could tackle, its price fell within our means.

"Do you have another house in you?" DC asked. I steeled myself for the project ahead. It would be a doozy, but we would make it perfect for us, and it would be our home for a long, long time.

PRACTICE MAKES PERFECT

Apart from making me an Olympic champion packer and mover, perhaps the most significant lesson that moving so many times has taught me is how much a home's floor plan defines how you live. If your kitchen doesn't open on to the family room, you won't interact with others much while you cook. Going from a wall closet to a walk-in closet to separate closets can be life changing, as can be having two sinks in a shared bathroom.

I read more when I have a pretty, cozy place to sit with good light, away from the television. I entertain more in houses that have a flowing floor plan. You don't discover this until you live it.

Though moving is a giant hassle, it offers a chance at finding a floor plan that better fits your lifestyle. Plus, a move, after you've blended once, offers a second chance to reevaluate and declutter, and gives you an organizing do-over. As you set up house for yourself and your partner again, you can improve systems that didn't work so well before, and create a place for all your well-edited belongings.

You also will see furnishings in a fresh way. Like mixing the letters in a word scramble, recombining furniture for new rooms enables you to see winning combinations you didn't see before, like how well a painting that you had in your living room works in the new master with the armoire your partner brought, or how your spouse's china cabinet can double as a bookcase.

In short, finding a home that supports the life you envision is perhaps the single best way you and your partner can celebrate this wonderful chance you get at doing it all again—but better.

So DC and I took one more good look at our furnishings—pieces I brought, he brought, and we bought—and shuffled them together like a worn deck of cards.

We went through the boxes we'd brought from our previous homes and lives that we hadn't yet opened. They contained items we hadn't needed. Possessions we'd once felt warmly toward now felt cold and unnecessary. Though we had more house to furnish, we still let go of more furnishings we either should have let go of in the first place, or simply couldn't see in our lives moving forward.

We did everything I've taught you to do in this book—one more time. But this time, confirming that old maxim "practice makes perfect," we did it even better. We picked our favorite things, set them in place, and worked in joint acquisitions. The abstract paintings on metal became the main statement in the family room; the traditional chairs we had re-covered in more contemporary fabric brought life to the master bedroom. We mixed what we had in fresh ways, creating combinations we hadn't seen before, probably because we had previously been too stuck on whose piece it was.

On Thanksgiving Day 2017, we moved into the Happier Yellow House. We cooked a turkey dinner for the two of us and ate by candlelight surrounded by moving boxes, our bodies tired but our hearts grateful.

The following year, we hosted Christmas at our house. Everyone came except Adam's family, who dropped in via FaceTime.

Gathered around our tree—decorated with a downsized and edited collection of his, mine, and our ornaments—were four of our children, three of their significant others, and two of our grandkids, including the new baby, Belle. That week, eleven people called the Happier Yellow House home.

They sat at the barstools and sprawled in the adjacent family room. The upstairs bedrooms were fully occupied, and the bathrooms were a blizzard. The kitchen looked just as chaotic and smelled just as delicious as I'd hoped. We put a leaf in the dining room table to extend it, which delighted me. We spread out holiday table linens that DC's late wife had chosen and loved, and that her kids found familiar. On those we set the china and silver that had been my mom's. We held hands around the table, as DC said grace and the dogs settled into their corners. My eyes got misty as they do at such times, as I reflected on how not so long ago I was alone, divorced and living in other people's houses. Then we went around the table and each person took a turn saying what he or she was grateful for.

When it came to my turn, I looked around the table at my beautiful crazy-quilt family, and said: "This."

We were home.

The Crazy Quilt at DC's and my wedding.
From left: Brett, Adam, DC, me, Paige, Marissa, and Alyssa.

Acknowledgments

Writing a book is a journey. Fortunately, it's one I don't have to take alone, because I couldn't. For the fact that this book, once an idea scrawled on the back of a grocery receipt, has made its way between these covers, I must credit a wide cast of colleagues, friends, and loved ones.

To the editors in newsrooms across America who see fit to print my column in their home and garden sections each week, thank you for keeping my ear to the ground and for making me come across in print better than I deserve to.

To my readers, thank you for teaching me more than I teach you, for calling me out when I've crossed a line (and even when I arguably haven't), and for coming along on my circuitous path to find home.

To my stellar agent, Linda Konner, thank you for your faith, wisdom, patient ear, and for helping me see the target before I shoot.

To my editor, Barbara Berger, who knows how to string disparate ideas together like pearls, thank you for helping me to shore when I felt as if I were swimming across the English Channel with an octopus. I am a better writer for having the good fortune to work with you again.

A round of applause also goes to the rest of the team at Sterling, from copyeditors to cover designers to publicists, who further tamed, dressed, and launched these pages.

To the many sources I tapped as I researched this book, thank you for sharing your time and expertise so generously. For their design expertise, sincerity, and friendship, and for taking my calls regardless of the time zone, I am especially indebted to Mark Brunetz, Elaine Griffin, and Christopher Grubb.

To the blended couples and families who brought the concepts in this book to life—Sara and Austin; Elaine and Mike; Kristin and Rich; Dean and Rebecca; John and Jason; and Sherry, Rachel, and Michael—thank you for trusting me with your personal journeys.

To Susan Beane, thank for getting out my credit card and making me put my profile on Match.com in March 2014, and thank you Match for whatever algorithms caused me to show up on DC's Daily Matches a week later. This book, and so much else, simply would not have happened otherwise.

To "the kids," which is easier than saying Adam, Amber, Brett, Tara, Alyssa, Paige, John, and Marissa, thank you for your resilience and for broadening and enriching my life in ways I could never have foreseen, and that includes being a constant font of material.

And not least, to the amazing Doug Carey, who read this book at every iteration, and who has been a terrific sport after losing whatever anonymity he once had, and who, though he will not deny that I am a dreadful companion when I am writing a book, loves and tolerates me still, and who mostly lets me put the furniture where I want: thank you, Darlin', for this crazy quilt life of ours.

Thank you, thank you. All of you.

Sources

Books

Brunetz, Mark. *Take the U Out of Clutter: The Last Clutter Book You'll Ever Need*. New York: Berkley, 2010.

Israel, Toby. *Some Place Like Home: Using Design Psychology to Create Ideal Places, 2nd ed*. Princeton, NJ: Design Psychology Press, 2010.

Loecke, John and Jason Oliver Nixon. *Prints Charming by Madcap Cottage: Create Absolutely Beautiful Interiors with Prints & Patterns*. New York: Abrams, 2017.

Lofas, Jeannette. *How to Be a Step Parent*. Wheeling, IL: Nightingale-Conant, 1989.

Lofas, Jeannette and Ruth Roosevelt. *Living in Step*. New York: McGraw-Hill, 1976.

Ridge, Brent and Josh Kilmer-Purcell. *Beekman 1802 Style: The Attraction of Opposites*. New York: Rodale Books, 2015.

Sassler, Sharon and Amanda Jayne Miller. *Cohabitation Nation: Gender, Class, and the Remaking of Relationships*. Oakland, CA: University of California Press, 2017.

West, Rebecca. *Happy Starts at Home: Getting the Life You Want by Changing the Space You've Got*. Bright House Books, 2016.

Whitman, Kimberly Schlegel. *Monograms for the Home: The Art of Making Your Mark*. Layton, UT: Gibbs Smith, 2015.

Studies

Harris, Alexander. "Storage Industry Statistics," SpareFoot Storage
Beat, March 11, 2019.

https://www.sparefoot.com/self-storage/news/1432-self-storage-
industry-statistics/

Livingston, Gretchen. "Four-in-Ten Couples Are Saying 'I Do,'
Again," Pew Research Center, November 14, 2014.

https://www.pewsocialtrends.org/2014/11/14/four-in-ten-
couples-are-saying-i-do-again/

Resources

The Center for Divorce Education
https://www.divorce-education.com/

Houzz
https://www.houzz.com/

National Association of Productivity & Organizing Professionals
https://www.napo.net/

Realtor.com
https://www.realtor.com/

The Step Family Foundation
http://www.stepfamily.org/

UGallery
https://www.ugallery.com/

Index